THEY WILL RUN AND NOT GROW WEARY

52 Devotions to Lighten Your Running Load

DAVID ALAN BLACK

Energion Publications
Gonzalez, FL
2019

Cover Design: Henry Neufeld
Print ISBNs:
ISBN10: 1-63199-690-8
ISBN13: 978-1-63199-690-0
Library of Congress Control Number: 2019940512

Energion Publications
P. O. Box 841
Gonzalez, FL 32560

energion.com
pubs@energion.com
850-525-3916

DEDICATION

To my children and grandchildren, who wait with patience and love for me to return from my races.

TABLE OF CONTENTS

PREFACE

I admit it. I don't always enjoy running. Especially when it's cold, windy, icy, stormy, humid or if I'm just plain tired. But neither life nor running is about convenience. It's about improving and overcoming.

People run for different reasons. Some run for causes. Most run for themselves — in a good sense. They're running from a destructive relationship. They're running to prove to themselves that they are worthy of another's love and affection. They're running to become fit. I run for many reasons I suppose. I think mostly I run for my wife Becky, in her honor, and to raise money to combat the disease that took her away from me. Someone has said that running isn't any different from grief. Both are hard. Neither gets easier. But both make you stronger.

I'm not trying to set new PRs every time I run. I just want to be out there with my fellow athletes. Your last race doesn't matter anymore. Each new starting line holds the promise of a small victory as you struggle against your limitations and push to the edge of your ability. You rediscover the will to win and the desire to finish.

How many miles have I put on this 67-year old body of mine since I began running 4 years ago? Who knows? Fifteen marathons – that's 393 miles right there – plus 17 half marathons (another 222 miles) and countless 5Ks, 10Ks, a few 10 Milers, 4 triathlons, and one 50K ultramarathon. Not to mention all the training runs I've done. I've made every mistake in the book as a runner. I've gone out too fast, eaten too much before a race, forgotten to bring water, tried something new on race day, refused to take rest days, forgotten to lube up, and trained on the wrong surface. Don't pretend it's never happened to you. Sometimes we need to adjust our running habits. At other times we just need friends to nudge us along. As fellow runners, you and I comprise a running *community*. We are there for each other. This book is my way of saying, "You can do this." As the writer of Hebrews reminds us (Hebrews 12:1), millions of people have gone before us. Each of them faced the same fear and insecurity as they ran their race. Each somehow learned to keep on going.

Personally, I find that running with other people helps me to get my mojo back. If you spend enough time around other runners, you find yourself saying things like, "A 31-mile trail run in winter conditions? At night? Where do I sign up?" Recognize that your motivation will always wax and wane. I'm pretty convinced that if we wait to feel like doing something we will probably get very little done. That said, drawing motivation from others isn't a bad idea. Having a good podcast, audio book, or running buddy can make a huge difference. This book is me standing at the starting line giving you a big High Five.

Humans were not made to stand still. We were created to move. The pace and distance is totally up to you. But sooner or later, the challenge will seem unconquerable. Maybe something you read here will help you to overcome those hurdles and ease your running burden. Family and running friends really do make a world of difference. Thank goodness we don't do this alone.

I

The Healing Power of Running

Have you ever wondered what makes a mountain peak so special? What makes it stand out? What makes summiting it such a glorious experience?

A peak stands out for one simple reason. It's surrounded by deep valleys and canyons.

When I first started running and mountain climbing, I did it for survival. I needed an avocation to keep my mind from dwelling on the loss and pain of my wife's death from cancer. My running and climbing are different now. I'm not running away from anything. I'm not running toward anything. I run because it's me. It's become an important part of my daily ritual, like washing the dishes or picking up the hair my Sheltie sheds.

Life today is calm and peaceful. I don't know, however, if I would have ever reached this point had it not been for the valleys. Becky's death has given me a new perspective on life and has broadened my understanding of the sovereignty of God. I've discovered that His sovereignty not only encompasses the tragedies in our lives but also our responses. It assures us that He is bigger than our problems and that indeed He leverages those problems to make our lives better. Becky's passing made me mourn, but it also helped me grow. I've been assigned a role (widower) for which I did not audition. Yet I, like many of you, have chosen to believe that God is working all of this toward some ultimate purpose.

Suffering cleanses the soul. Through suffering we are like the phoenix, reborn. And we will keep being reborn until we can soar no more.

2

ADVENTURE IS YOUR FRIEND

I can still see it today. I am descending a 4,000-meter peak in the Alps. More than once I slip and fall on the ice. Thankfully, I'm roped to my mountain guide. Two thoughts are going through my brain and only two: *Will I make it down safely? Will it have been worth it?* Have you ever had moments like that? Moments when you question your sanity? Moments that make you wonder why a grown man over 60 would attempt something as ridiculously difficult as climbing the Alps? Moments when you are confronted with a seemingly impossible task and yet somehow you pushed through? Did I make it down? Yes, thanks to my guide and the One who created the Alps. Was it worth it? $25,000 was raised for UNC Cancer Hospital. Yes, I'd say it was worth it.

The question you must ask yourself is, amid your personal journey on this planet, is God calling you to do something impossible? Is He asking you to find a challenge and then go for it, even if you fail in the end? Life is too short to live a dull, mundane life. My heart yearns for adventure and mystery. I love stepping into the great unknown and finding out what's there. Past adventures are just that — past. It's time for me to move on from outworn memories and pursue the next goal.

Do you remember what it was like to start college or get married? The butterflies and the curiosity? I recall training for my first marathon. Then, 8 marathons later, I was training for my first 31-mile race. It's like I was reaching down and touching my soul, like I did when I found the Lord, or welcomed my firstborn into the world, or summited my first 14,000-er in the Rockies, or published my first book, or finished my 17th ministry trip to Ethiopia. In any event, I'm eager for new adventures to begin. I'm enticed by their distance and difficulty. I'm anxious to see how well I'll do.

Need a new adventure, my friend? Just step outside. But make sure you've got your running (or climbing) shoes on.

3
PLOTTING
THE PATH

In case you didn't know it, I'm a Greek professor. Are there any comparisons between running a marathon and learning how to read New Testament Greek? Much, in every way. Here are some things I've learned from these two disciplines that I believe will benefit you in any undertaking in life:

1) *Don't start anything without first examining your motives.* It all begins with desire. I took Greek in college because it was required for graduation. I had no idea that I would fall in love with the language. I sort of stumbled into my career, if you will. Some of you may be like me. You were shocked when you took Greek (or biology, or accounting), only to discover that you really love what you're doing. So, make sure you're motivated, or you'll never get past square one.

2) *You need to plan and prepare.* Because sooner or later it will happen. A 5K becomes routine. So does a 10K, and even a half. You begin to think the unthinkable. *A marathon? Am I really up to it?* You can't simply go from a 5K to a marathon. A marathon is, by definition, a race that requires a training program. So it is with Greek. Are you ready to tackle a difficult subject like Greek? Can you devote sufficient time each week for study? Have you carefully chosen your "trainer" and your "training program" — that is, a teacher and a textbook? Not all textbooks are created equal. Teachers can be helpful, but they can also get in the way. You can't be half-hearted with your planning and preparation.

3) *You won't get anywhere without self-discipline.* Nearly all of us find that running requires more effort than we ever thought possible. With Greek, it's easy to burn out after a couple of chapters. Some days you feel like you just can't go on. On those days the real test is not in your mind but in your soul. All you can do on those days is just keep putting one foot in front of the other. Both running and learning Greek will teach you something about yourself. Some days you're convinced that the world should make allowances for you. You want everything to be easy. You want all the traffic lights to be green. You want to be in the fastest line at the grocery store. But life doesn't always work that way. Being a runner often means going to the very edges of your ability and strength. Greek students find that small victories make all the difference in the world. You master one chapter and then the next one. You know that somewhere out there is a finish line. As you keep your eyes on the goal, somehow you're able to keep those arms pumping and legs churning.

4) *Remember that you're not alone.* The running community is just that — a community of fellow runners of all sizes, shapes, and abilities who are more than willing to help you get to the finish line. In my Greek classes, students are encouraged to request personal tutoring if they feel they need it. Some students enjoy studying with a study partner. Having someone to share the load with you builds confidence. My story as a runner is largely a story about the people I've met along the way, people who have shared their joys with me, laughed with me, and tutored me. This is not just true of me but of everyone who runs.

5) *Finally, be aware of the risks.* Simply having the desire to run a marathon doesn't guarantee that you'll be successful. Simply wanting to take Greek doesn't mean that you will finish the class or master the textbook. We are often "interrupted" by life. I remember when I was teaching Greek every Monday night in my local church. My wife was one of my best students. She was acing all the quizzes and exams. She had always wanted to take Greek with me and now

was her chance. Then the chemo kicked in and she became too weak to continue her studies. One thing I admired so much about Becky was that she never looked back at what might have been. When I first enrolled in Greek at Biola, I lasted exactly three weeks before dropping. Then I discovered that Moody Bible Institute had a Greek course that was taught on my level, and the rest, as they say, is history. If you've had a false start, that's okay. Take a break, then get back in line. If you see me running a marathon, you'll probably smile. Don't be surprised at the sight of my plodding style and persistence. And don't expect me to ever stop smiling.

I love what I do. I love my running life. As slow and silly as I may look, I'm having the time of my life. Day by day, moment by moment, I'm adding to the mosaic of who I am and who I want to be. Every day I am closer to becoming the person my Creator wants me to be. Nothing of value in life comes easy. We slay our challenges one dragon at a time.

4

BALANCE
BODY AND SOUL

I've read and benefitted from *Every Body Matters* by Gary Thomas, who is writer-in-residence at a church in Houston. Here are a few takeaways:

☐ It's not about obtaining a "holy" body; it's about coming to terms with gluttony (over-eating) and sloth (laziness when it comes to caring for our bodies).

☐ "[O]vereating and overindulgence lead to deprivation" (p. 22).

☐ Good health is an ongoing battle but one worth fighting.

☐ We can't only live from the chin up; we are a combination of body, mind, and spirit.

☐ A healthy body is a fit home for a vibrant spirit.

☐ By caring for our bodies we honor and love God.

☐ It's not just how much we eat but what we eat.

☐ "Hunger is a sensation, nothing more. It should never become my Lord and Master" (p. 58).

☐ It's never right to disparage people because they are over-weight.

- "The Body Mass Index (BMI) isn't found in Scripture" (p. 80).

- There may be spiritual reasons for why we gain weight.

- "[F]itness isn't [just] about avoiding disease; it's about avoiding frailty" (p. 114).

- Good health is not about good looks but about being fit for active service to God.

- "[M]otivation is 99 percent of the battle" (p. 160).

Totally agree! We should all pursue good health to the extent we are able. For me, exercise isn't merely a physical or biological move, but a kingdom action. Through exercise we'll never overturn the curse of the fall. In fact, good health can sometimes get in the way of seeing God's grace and the need for Him. We can get so busy with exercise that it's easy to forget or ignore the beauty that God wants to create in our inner being. How to obtain this balance? Don't ask me, because I don't have the foggiest idea. I'm still trying to figure this one out. But one thing is clear: If I'm to continue to do kingdom work, I need to stay in good physical condition.

On the other hand, let me state emphatically: our wounds (spiritual, emotional, psychological, physical, etc.) do not disqualify us from ministry. In fact, God often uses our weaknesses to display His overarching power. For Paul, his "disabilities" were badges of honor. God's strength was perfected in his imperfections.

Remember that. You're not the best athlete out there. You never will be. Just stay focused on being you. The key is to just stick with it.

5

LEARN TO REST, NOT QUIT

Resting is as much a part of a good training program as running is, or so I'm told. When I talk to people who used to run but have since stopped for whatever reason (usually lack of interest or commitment), it makes me really sad to hear them say they were frustrated by their lack of progress. Never compare your running with anyone else's. Dedication is a personal thing. It means when you start something, you carry it through to its conclusion. It means not giving up and not giving in. It means making every run and every race a mystery. My advice to them would be: Give yourself permission to relax. You might get more enjoyment out of the sport that way. After running now for several years, I'm blessed to say that I never feel that running is an obligation. I look forward to my walks/runs/climbs/races. Learn to respect your body. Is it telling you to exercise? Then go out the door and get busy. There's so much to enjoy along the way, from improved fitness to better health. Enjoy each new experience that comes your way. Enjoy being the athlete you're becoming. But never forget to rest.

6

PERSEVERE TO THE END

I doubt that the apostle Paul was a runner or that he even knew about New Balance or Hoka. But he knew enough about athletics to write these words:

You've all been to the stadium and seen the athletes race. Everyone runs; one wins. Run to win.

Then he added:

All good athletes train hard. They do it for a gold medal that tarnishes and fades. You're after one that's gold eternally. I don't know about you, but I'm running hard for the finish line. I'm giving it everything I've got. No sloppy living for me! I'm staying alert and in top condition. I'm not going to get caught napping, telling everyone else all about it and then missing out myself
(The Message)

Even I, your ultimate non-runner-turned-runner, can find myself caught up in the same passion that Paul expressed in 1 Corinthians 9:24-27. Did he train hard? So do I. Did he run hard for the finish line? Me too. Did he stay in top condition? Ummm ..... But you get my drift. There are so many reasons we Christians give for quitting the race we're in. Our obstacles range from bad habits to lousy attitudes to fear or our lack of transparency. There will be times when we will want to give up or slacken the pace. As Paul says, we can get caught napping. While telling everyone else how to have a successful life, we fail to have one ourselves. That's why Jesus said His life is an example for us. He persevered to the very end.

How can we have the "life" of Christ on a daily basis? There is no simple answer. Remember, we are all real people with real weaknesses who fall short of God's standards on almost a daily basis. I pondered this question as I sat on the front porch with Sheba, and no kidding, the Lord taught me a lesson from my dog. Though she is independent and autonomous (she can run off any time she likes), she's learned that I can be relied on to care for her needs (food, water, shelter, attention). In a word, she trusts me. I find that learning to trust God is just like that. In the midst of agonizing over our insecurities and uncertainties, God is there to support those who trust in Him. "Those who trust in the Lord will find new strength. They will soar high on wings like eagles. They will run and not grow weary. They will walk and not faint" (Isaiah 40:31). "Yes," He says. "I will love you completely, no strings attached, even when you're unable to love back." I know this isn't a particularly cosmic observation, but when our horizontal relationships seem to be going off the rails, there's probably something missing in our vertical relationship. In a nutshell, lack of trust is at the root of so many of our problems. Moving mountains isn't something we can do on our own. But we've got every chance in the world if we trust God to do it.

It's one thing to start a race and quit. It's another thing altogether to go the distance and finish it. Let's "run to win," shall we?

7

WE'RE ALL WINNERS

Marathoning is something I will do for the rest of my life. In the past I've trained feverishly, averaging well over 100 miles of training per month. Now I'm trying to get away from a focus on miles to a focus on enjoyment. Theologians might call this the "already-not-yet" paradox. You're already a runner, and yet it seems like you're always adjusting your standards and goals, trying to *become* the runner you want to be. Your success is of little consequence to anybody but you. Eventually, your joy isn't that of a rugged athlete. It's the joy children feel when they run through a lawn sprinkler on a hot summer day.

Entering a race is such a great experience. You will never, ever forget the first time you cross a finish line. You realize that your best is good enough, even if you finish dead last. It's being a runner that matters, not how fast or how far you can run. The road is there, right in front of you, inviting you to enjoy all the miracles it holds. When I race I have zero chance of winning, but ample opportunities to be victorious. My goal is very simple: Take that one final step across the finish line.

Dear friend, every step in life takes us closer to where we want to go. With every step we discover something new about God's will for our life. It's as though the act of running drives something buried deep within us. It is knowing that we have accepted and rejected the limitations of life, and that makes all of us winners.

8

LOOKING BACK
TO GO FORWARD

*Therefore, having so vast a cloud of witnesses sur-
rounding us, and throwing off everything that
hinders us and especially the sin that so easily entangles us, let us keep running with endurance the race
set before us, fixing our attention on Jesus, the pioneer
and perfecter of faith, who, in view of the joy set before him, endured the cross, disregarding its shame,
and has sat down at the right hand of the throne of
God* (Hebrews 12:1-2, ISV).

I once published an excruciatingly boring, long-winded, pe-
dantic, and obfuscatory essay on this passage that I don't expect
any of you to actually read unless you're into suffering. So I'll try
to give you a cook's tour of the kitchen here and hopefully inspire
you to get into this passage for yourself sometime. You know, it
truly is a masterpiece. The text begins with a very strong Greek
transitional marker — *toigaroun* — which is found only here and
1 Thessalonians 4:8 in the entire New Testament. It's a "therefore,"
but a *strong* "therefore." The reason the author uses it here, I believe,
is that before he calls on his readers to run *their* race, he wants to
be sure they reflect deeply on the Old Testament personages he's
already pointed out in Chapter 11. The application for us today
might be this: As you run your race, who are those people in your
life, now in heaven, who set an example for you in terms of running
with endurance? And this is just where Becky Black comes into

play. If there was anybody I know who bore a consistent testimony to the faithfulness of God in her life, it was Becky. She lived her life of faith, and she lived it well. And now, Paul says, it's my turn. It's time for *me* to remain firm in faith through the sufferings I face.

So how do I do that? Notice the structure of this passage. There's one main command here and only one: "Let us keep on running with endurance the race set before us." If your Bible has more than one "let us" (the NASB and ESV have two, the NIV three), sorry, folks, but that's too much lettuce. Here's how the text unpacks itself:

Therefore, let us keep on running with endurance the race set before us
- ☐ <u>having</u> so vast a cloud of witnesses surrounding us,

- ☐ <u>throwing off</u> everything that hinders us and especially the sin that so easily entangles us,

- ☐ <u>fixing our attention</u> on Jesus, the pioneer and perfector of faith.

The underlined words are all participles in Greek, telling us how we are to keep on running with endurance. We can thus (*toigaroun!*) immediately see the author's main point – running *our* race with endurance – as well as his qualifications of the "race":

- ☐ By knowing that others have finished the race, the present generation of runners can expect to complete it.

- ☐ No runner, however, can hope to attain the goal without getting rid of hindrances and an abhorrence of personal sin.

- ☐ The runner must look to Jesus, the pioneer and perfecter of faith.

Teaching this text? Here's a possible outline:

- ☐ Our Encouragement ("having so vast a cloud of witnesses")

- ☐ Our Entanglements ("throwing off everything that hinders us")

- ☐ Our Example ("fixing our attention on Jesus")

I am here to tell you: There *is* a way to run our race successfully. First, there's nothing quite like drawing encouragement from those who have already completed their race. Remember them. Recall their example. Emulate the outcome of their faith. Be intentional about it. Stop by their graveside. Read Scripture that reminds you of them. Speak of them often to your kids and grandkids. The heroes of Hebrews 11 are the life and breath and strength of the church. The kingdom advances in small feats of courage performed by people who've simply been faithful where they were planted.

Secondly, your life is too precious to waste on pettiness, greed, selfishness, pride, sloth — or anything "that hinders us." The voyage into the kingdom of God is a grand but difficult adventure. It's like running a marathon. Imagine what would happen if you had to tackle a marathon dressed in a coat of armor. Recently I began a race with a tank top, t-shirt, and jacket. I ended the race with my tank top only. *Strip it away!* says the author of Hebrews. And that includes the sin(s) in our lives. Change is always possible through the Christ who indwells us.

Finally and ultimately, our race is not about the cloud of witnesses or our easily-entangling sins. It's about a Person, a safe place to be sequestered, a soul-Lover who understands the journey because He completed it Himself. I grew up looking to men. I respected and loved my pastors and leaders immensely, probably too much. You see, there comes a time when we must take responsibility for our own spiritual development. I am suggesting this: Listen to sermons, yes, but study the Bible for *yourself* more. Healthy people do not blindly follow other people. They reject the whole pedestal thing. What they look for in their leaders is humility and transparency. Because, honestly, no matter who we look at, we will ultimately be disappointed. Corrie ten Boom, one of my favorite theologians, put it this way:

- ☐ Look inside and be depressed.

- ☐ Look outside and be distressed.

- ☐ Look to Him and be at rest.

If you, my friend, are facing the silent scream of pain today, if you've lost a spouse (or are about to), or if you're just tired of running your race, please, please remember that, though terrors in this life surely await us, life is still worth living — celebrating even — if we keep our focus on Jesus.

9
EVERYONE IS CALLED

Once, while running a marathon, I saw a team of volunteers from a church passing out cups of gummy bears in Jesus' name. They had a corner on the market too, since there were plenty of other volunteers blessing us with cups of cold water. Believe me, at mile 8, these "bearers" of energy were just what the doctor ordered. But I have to ask myself: In all of my running, why is this the first time I've seen a church out on a race course? Serving others can only be done when we begin to realize that the gathering exists for the going.

I have a special empathy for people trying to find their place in the body of Christ. But let's not forget to consider simple, towel-and-basin ministries such as this one. Simply put, serving others in Jesus' name is what we do with who we are in Christ. Every believer has been called to serve in the kingdom of God. Markus Barth reminds us that the entire church "is the *clergy* appointed by God for a ministry to and for the world" (*Ephesians*, p. 479). This is the highest calling possible. Paul says that the body grows into the Head through every joint or connection point. How different it would be to us runners if we saw church after church doing such simple acts of service. We would welcome the God-given concern being expressed. This is why, significantly, the goal of leadership in the church is to get every member of the body relating to the Head for himself or herself. The leading servants will do this primarily in the context of exercising their own spiritual gifts. The church needs these specially gifted leaders, but the call of God also comes to every believer who has ears to hear — even if this means that they stand in the oppressive heat and humidity passing out gummy bears in the name of their King.

Church, I'm convinced we can do this. Friend, I hope that when you get to the end of your life, you will breathe a huge sigh of relief and thanksgiving. I hope you will have discovered that God is good at being God. I hope you will have discovered that He was willing to use you in normal, everyday circumstances to be a blessing to others in His name. We don't have to be superstars. We're probably better at just being normal folk anyway.

10

YOU BE YOU,
LET THEM BE THEM

Every semester I give out tons of A plusses. But I also give out Bs and an occasional C or even D. I tell my students, if you think you have to get an A in this class to please your professor, you're in the wrong class. In college I got Bs in several classes, especially if they had anything to do with philosophy, math, or logic. I stink at those subjects. But I tried as hard as I could. I am incredibly blessed to have finished a master's degree, not to speak of a doctorate. It's not like I studied or anything in high school. (You wouldn't either if you grew up in Hawaii.) Deciding to become a real student (i.e., somebody who actually studies) was the first step toward me becoming a teacher. I had completely run out of excuses *not* to study. Likewise, a couple of years ago, I decided to take up the sport of running. Without being aware of it at the time, I realize now that Becky's passing was a reminder of my own mortality and made me a little more health conscious.

There are, of course, many reasons for running. For elite runners, it's their bread and butter. For me, it's a hobby. They'll do their thing and I'll do mine (much, much slower of course). Either way, running is a great sport. Today, there are well over 100 marathons in the U.S. alone. I'll pass on most of them, but before I end up permanently affixed to my front porch, I'd still like to do some of the majors, including Chicago, New York, and Athens. These are known as World Marathon Majors, but to me they're just races that have oodles of runners in them, and I like running in crowds.

So take courage, my friend. "The glory of God," wrote Irenaeus (an early church father), "is man fully functioning." That's true whether you're trying your hardest to get a good grade in a class or just trying to finish a road race. For now, I simply rejoice at being healthy and of (relatively) sane mind. All of that will change one day, of course. But even then, I suppose that one can still find the "peace that passes all understanding."

11

SHOWING UP, DARING GREATLY

For me, the best part about being outdoors is fellowshipping with my Creator. My running brings me closer to Him. Over and over again I can hear Him saying, "My grace is enough for you, Dave" (2 Corinthians 12:9). At the end of the day, I know that He will be with me through thick and thin, enabling me to keep on taking one step after the other.

I feel like the breakthrough moment in my Christian life came when I realized that anything we do as Jesus-followers has the potential of glorifying God, even if it's washing dishes or running a road race. (I do both of these activities frequently.) This might sound revolutionary, but I believe it's absolutely true. Running is a "ministry" of mine every bit as much as teaching is. The truth is that, as Christians, we find our greatest pleasure when we are doing what God created us to be and do without ever comparing ourselves to anyone else. In Greek, the verbs "serve," "minister," and "worship" are closely related. My goal in life is to serve and worship God in everything I do. This means, for one thing, that I no longer separate the "sacred" from the "secular" parts of my life. Being a Christian is not about dying to our natural gifts or God-given desires and joys. It's about living the life He's given us to the max. Every day, through my running, God is teaching me more and more about who I am in Him. It's not about running fast or about running slow. I run not because I want to but because I have to. I teach for the same reason. Yes, teaching is my "job," my "vocation," but it's oh so much more than that. I know of no other way to live than to teach. Likewise, I know of no other way to exist apart from being active, as long as God allows me to be active.

Being a runner is so much like being a Christian. You begin at the starting line and then each step takes you closer to the finish line. There is always a goal in your relentless forward progress. Not only do you want to see what you're capable of accomplishing in life, in your heart of hearts you want to see how God works through your life to bless others. But here's the clincher: At some point in your race, pain becomes your companion. It becomes part of the journey. Sometimes the pain is relatively minor, and at other times it is practically unbearable. But pain always comes to us eventually. Fortunately, Christianity teaches us how to suffer. Running in the midst of pain is a crash course in perseverance and gratitude. In those moments, when you are struggling, when your limits are being tested, you sense that the Lord is with you in a special way. Heaven seems to come down and touch the earth.

C. S. Lewis once put it this way: "If one could run without getting tired, I don't think that one would often want to do anything else." I love road races, not only because of the fantastic comradery, but because they remind us that we, yes *we,* can do this, that we are capable of so much more than we know. In my running life, I try not to live with regrets. "I should have done this or that." Nope. Learn from your mistakes, Dave, but don't dwell on the past. Life vacillates between peaks and valleys. Get used to it. The one constant is the Lord. Every day, God is teaching me more about who I am and who He wants me to be. It's awesome to know that while cycling or running or cooking or teaching or cleaning the house He's right there with me. He created me this way. He created me to celebrate the disciplined, physically hard-working lifestyle. I am meant to be fully alive, fully alive in Christ. I am adamant, therefore, that being a Christian doesn't mean a joyless existence.

"When I run, I feel His pleasure," said Eric Liddell in the movie *Chariots of Fire.* What are *you* doing to feel His pleasure, my friend? Our primary role is to find God's will for our lives and then

22

pursue it with all we have. And this "divining" God's will for our lives is not exclusive to one denomination, gender, ethnicity, etc. Each of us can know God if we truly seek Him. After all, He's the one who both designed the race course and finished it (Hebrews 12:2). Our only job is to look to Him, "the pioneer and perfecter of faith."

12

KEEP MOVING FORWARD

Let's talk about motivation for a second. Here are some reasons that come to my mind of why I think I've been able to stay motivated to keep running for so long.

- When I run, my right brain is engaged. My mind is re-energized and the creative juices are really flowing. Which is one reason I can't wait to blog after a race.

- When I run, my spirit is engaged. I am free to soar and dream even bigger dreams.

- When I run, my body is engaged. My stress levels are reduced, and my attitude is better after every run.

- When I run, I become a "complete" person. Mind, body, and spirit are all engaged, together. You're learning about connections you thought were never there. In fact, verses like Romans 12:1 begin to make better sense to you ("present your *bodies* as a living sacrifice unto God").

- When I run, I feel myself being drawn closer and closer to my Creator and Savior. I'm always conscious of His presence, realizing that He is the One who gives me strength.

- Finally, when I run, natural chemicals called endorphins relax me and help my body to cope with all of its aches and pains.

It's really no more complicated than that. To stay motivated, you simply have to have good reasons to do what you're doing. When I took Greek, I fell in love with the language. Yes, it was challenging. After all, it was my very first foreign language. But when Greek clicked, everything else seemed to click along with it. I found my "niche" in life, so to speak. And, 43 years later, I am enjoying the classroom as much today as I did when I first entered it.

I am an adult-onset athlete. I believe that having an active lifestyle is the only responsible course of action for a 67-year old who takes Romans 12:1 seriously. I owe it to my family to stay in shape for as long as possible. Moreover, I've found the running community to be one of the most compassionate, supportive, giving, and understanding communities I've ever been involved with. Had I known how rich my life would have been as a runner, I would have put my running shoes on much earlier. Staying active is really a matter of faith. It's part of our stewardship responsibility before our Creator. The people you see running 5Ks on the weekend aren't any more talented or gifted than you are. They haven't suddenly discovered the secret to happiness. They aren't any different from you and me. They're just normal, everyday people who've discovered that running is a whole-being activity. It nourishes your mind, your body, and your spirit.

When you stand at the starting line of a marathon, your goal that day is to complete 26.2 miles. The difference between success and failure is as simple as taking the next step. I imagine that's how all of life is. "Wherever you are, be all there, and live to the hilt what you consider to be the will of God for your life" (Jim Elliott). Jim Elliott did just that and entered heaven "through gates of splendor." The truth is, every step in life is important. Every step takes us a little bit closer to who we want to become. Every step reveals some new God-given potential. My hope and dream is that you will find your "niche" in life and then pursue it with all the gusto you can.

13

THE RACE IS MARKED BY THE MAKER

You have to have a goal going into your races. And, once you set such goals, you accept the risk of failing to meet them. Unlike a daily jog, during a race you put everything on the line. You're willing to find out what you're made of. Once you pin that number on your shirt, you're a racer!

If you look at the course map for any race, you'll notice three things:

1) The course is marked out for the runners. It is intended to be a track or path kept by them. Runners don't design the race course. And they don't have the luxury of going off course either. Their job is to run within the boundaries. That's their duty.

2) One look at a course map and you quickly realize just how much effort is going to be required of you on race day. You can already see your muscles straining, your body kicking it into high gear. Nothing can be accomplished unless you give it your best shot. Running a race requires concentration and vigorous effort. Nothing less will do on race day.

3) The course by its very nature is progressive. You don't cross the finish line immediately. You finish mile 1, then mile 2, then mile 3, until you reach the 26.2 mile marker.

The image of a race is a common one in the New Testament, and so I can't help applying these observations to my own Christian life. First of all, God has a very specific plan for my life. It's been marked out by Him, and He intends for me to finish it. To diverge from it would be foolish and perilous. I have to constantly ask myself before beginning my day, "What is God's appointed task for me today? At what stage of the course am I on?" Obligation is laid upon me to finish my course.

Secondly, continual effort is required if I am to finish my race. Anything worth doing in life requires effort. The Christian life demands constant concentration and the utmost energy.

Finally, is my Christian life one of continual advance? Am I a more faithful follower of Jesus this year than I was last year? Am I making progress? Of course, our progress will be marred by failures and imperfections. One can be blameless without being perfect. Racing is all about putting forth an honest effort. And, one day, I'll answer for my choices.

Fellow believers, let's oppose the temptation to become lazy in the Christian life. Let's challenge the mentality that says "It's too hard." Let's stop lying about ourselves and using our weaknesses and imperfections to keep us from pursuing wholeheartedly the will of God. But be prepared for a struggle. We've invented a thousand excuses to take the easy way out.

According to Scripture, no real disciple is content with the level of spirituality to which they have attained. Friend, no one can run your race for you. But be sure of this: The pioneer and perfecter of faith will enable you to finish your course, meet faithfully every duty, and overcome every trial.

Oh my stars, what a great way to live life!

14

BUILT FOR
COMMUNITY

In my Greek classes we discuss words and how they take on meaning. It's all part of an effort to make classes practical and motivational. At the same time, there's nothing easy about lexical analysis. Much of it is undoing damage. Take the well-known and much-discussed fallacy of etymologizing — determining a word's meaning by its parts. For example, some insist that a New Testament church is "called out" from the world — separate, if you will — based on the etymology of the Greek word *ekklesia,* which is comprised of two parts — *ek,* "out of," and *kaleō,* "I call." Hence the church is a "called out" organism. It is to be *different* from the world. And believers are to separate themselves *from* the world.

In New Testament usage, however, the word *ekklesia* never quite had this meaning of "called out ones." Normally it was used to describe a group of people that had something in common. At times this group met, and then it was an *ekklesia.* At other times it wasn't meeting *per se,* but even then it was an *ekklesia.* This term was used in contrast to *ochlos* — a term that describes a group of people that have come together and have nothing in common. *Ochlos* is often glossed as "crowd" in English, and that is indeed a very good rendering. How, then, should we translate *ekklesia* into English? When I pose this question in my classes, I usually get several excellent responses: "gathering," "assembly," "congregation," and the like. All of these are fine, but none of them in my opinion captures the essence of what a New Testament *ekklesia* is. I prefer the term "community." Church is not simply a group of just *any* people, and it is most certainly not a building. Instead, I like to think of a church as a space in which *all of us* are ministering, praying, preaching, teaching, singing, caring, loving — a family if you will. Our motto might be: "We're all in this together. So let's do it together." This is the community to which we, as followers of Jesus, are giving ourselves with our whole hearts. This is our "church" — a diverse, global, caring paean of praise to our Creator, Redeemer, Sustainer, Lord, Master, and only true Senior Pastor.

As you know, in recent years I've become part of a similar community, one known simply as the "running community." The similarities between this community and the "church" are legion. As soon as I began running competitively, I knew I had joined the ranks of hundreds and thousands of other runners. From my very first race this sense of community became instilled deep within my psyche. Even as a novice runner, I knew I was not alone. Every experienced runner remembers when they were a beginner just like you, and so they are eager to reach out to the newbies among them. You soon have a group of running friends you look to for advice — where to buy the best running shoes, how to train properly, how to avoid injuries, how to handle anxiety before a big race.

Being part of this community helps each of us become a better runner. As runners, we value what we can become and not simply what we look like. We are not defined by our age, our t-shirt size, our weight, or our medallions (or lack of them). We are all fiercely independent and pursue individual goals, and yet paradoxically we truly believe that we are *all in this together,* and it shows. Just show up to any race and observe the runners.

I'm not in the least surprised, therefore, to find similarities between a running community and a community that defines itself on the basis of the traditional creedal values of faith, hope, and love. Both runners and Christians have a lot in common. For one thing, we both ask silly questions. A Christian in a bookstore asks the salesperson: "I'm looking for a Bible for my mother, but I'm not sure who the author is." A novice runner asks you, "How far is your next 5K race?" As you can see, both novice runners and novice

Christians have a lot to learn. We are people who pursue excellence and who seek to be dedicated to something wholeheartedly and to give ourselves to some project without any reservations whatsoever. Our actions are always impelled by some good we want to attain. And to achieve our goals, we often have to endure suffering and pain. An athletic race is a place where we discover strength and faith and courage we never knew we possessed. We are *runners*. It doesn't matter how fast we run or how far we run. It doesn't matter whether we are running in our very first race or have been running for fifty years.

During a recent 5K race I met an athletic-looking young man who was pushing his infant child in a stroller. We had finished the race about the same time. I knew he could have run much faster had he not been pushing a baby carriage. He told me something I'll never forget. He said, "Sometimes having the best time at a race has nothing to do with how fast you ran." I will remember that until the day I die. I wish I could have given him "The World's Greatest Runner Award" that day. Folks, the Christian life is a race we run *together*. It's no different in the running community. "Hey guys. I've got a hip labral tear. Anybody had any experience with this?" Or (in the church), "As a mom, I have a tremendous sense of responsibility to teach my children about truth and grace and God. Should I *make* my children read the Bible? What do you think?" The point is: We are there *for each other*.

As I've gotten older, I've found my priorities changing. I find myself wanting richer, more intimate and complex relationships with my family and friends. Like women, men have a primal need for closeness. We were created for relationships. Men discover that as they move into middle and older age they also move from com-petition to connecting. The best corporate managers are those who foster networks of connectivity. The best professors, too, prize be-ing hands-on guides and mentors to their students, and not only disseminators of information. Before Becky died, she was the one who did most of the connecting with our kids on an emotional level. But as I've come into my own as a widower, I've come to a realization that emotionally connecting with my kids and grandkids is deeply enriching. One of the things that my loss of Becky did for me personally was to make me value and cherish my family more. It's like taking the barnacles off. *Now* is the time in life to enjoy my family. The real ideal of manhood here is "servant-leader" in which we men discover our nurturing side. The apostle Paul had a lot to say about love. He knew that love is not blind. Nobody is perfect, least of all those closest to us. What is necessary in love is the ability to see others as God sees us. And to love others correctly, we must first love ourselves. The self must first be strong and whole before we can offer true and lasting love to others. Love is a positive sum game where both sides can and should win.

Which brings me back to the notion of community. An athletic team has goals that far surpass the aspirations of its individual players. And that's true of all of life. As I look forward to the winter of my life, I want to be a man who joins the "I" to the "we," whether that's in my family, my church, my profession, my mission work, and even my hobbies. Saying I want to do this is quite easy. Becoming the self I want to become is quite difficult. But every healthy relationship at least makes an attempt to meld the "I" with the "we."

15

A RUNNER IS A RUNNER NO MATTER HOW FAST OR SLOW, OLD OR YOUNG

I am a runner.
It doesn't matter how untalented I am.
I am a runner.
It doesn't matter how un-divine
my running skills are.
I am a runner.
It doesn't matter that I'm old and gray.
I am a runner.

The fact is, many people today are experiencing the joy of running miles they once thought they could never run. I'm one of them. I wasn't always. Running was always for other people. Now, for me, nothing matches the feeling of standing at the starting line with a few hundred or even a few thousand other runners with nothing better to do that day except to make our way to the finish line. The best thing of all is knowing that I'm running with people who share my goals and values and who are all going in the same direction. You don't have to be a professional to run. You don't have to be a 10-minute miler. Old or young, fast or slow, professional or amateur, heavy or slim, "abled" or disabled, you, like me, can bask in the glory of race day success.

16

RUN THROUGH
SELF-DOUBT

Christian baptism is one of the seven marks of a New Testament church. This topic often comes up in my Gospels class when we look at the participles "baptizing" and "teaching" in Matthew 28:19. Clearly Jesus intended for water to come before wisdom. In the New Testament book of Acts, if you got saved, you got wet, in that order and often without much of a pause between the two events. Of course, my human logic tells me that Jesus has things backwards here. Shouldn't we instruct new converts in the faith and test the genuineness of their conversion before we allow them to be baptized? Makes good sense to me. And indeed, in places like East Africa, baptism is postponed for months, sometimes even up to a year, before converts are allowed to enter the waters of baptism. The only problem with this is that Jesus' order is baptism *then* teaching, and we have no right to amend the Master's priorities. We can't simply ignore what our Lord taught and indeed what the early church practiced.

The reason I called my chapter on baptism "*Christian* Baptism" in my book *Seven Marks of a New Testament Church* is because the earliest believers were mostly Jews who were well acquainted with daily ablutions and ceremonial washings. Christian baptism is unique in that (1) it is no longer self-administered and (2) it is unrepeatable. Converts don't baptize themselves and, when they are baptized, they don't ever have to repeat the act. I also suggest in my book that baptism in the book of Acts was a *public* act whenever possible.

I recall once reading about a church in Africa that baptizes new converts in the ocean. The candidate is literally thrown into a wave "in the name of the Father," at which point he or she is washed back to shore. (Can't you just picture that?) But it gets even better. The church leaders quickly pick up the now drenched convert and throw him or her into another wave "in the name of the Son." This is repeated a third time, "in the name of the Spirit." (Interestingly, as a lifelong surfer I've noticed that waves often come in sets of three.) The point apparently is not simply to emphasize the name of the Triune God. In baptizing people this way, converts are given a tactile baptismal experience that initiates them into the *struggle* of the Christian faith. "Hey, follow Jesus if you want to, but man, it's going to cost you!" I'm reminded of Paul's famous "encouraging message" to the believers in Asia Minor. After urging them to stick with their new-found faith and not give up, he said, "Anyone signing up for the kingdom of God has to go through hard times" (Acts 14:22).

I can't resist the temptation to draw yet another analogy to running in a race. In many ways, that first race was your easiest. After all, that's where you got your very first PR. Now that you are a "runner," however, the real struggle begins. Some days you just can't get out of bed to do it. You struggle with willpower, with sore feet, with aching quads, with lack of motivation. I'm not proud to admit it, but I have these struggles almost every day. As Unknown once said, "My sweatpants smell like give up." Life can be hard. Actually, life *is* hard. On race day my legs often feel like they weigh 200 pounds each. You have to learn to push the doubts aside and just keep on going. And I will. Because I'm hooked. Even with all my self-doubts and infirmities, I am a dedicated runner. My race times might not make salacious headlines, but for me they are symbols of victory. I'm overwhelmed by the joy of it all, despite all the "hard times." Racing, like life, is just plain tough work. But the task is made easier when I consider that everything I have is a gift from God, freely bestowed, so I should freely give it back in return

(Matthew 10:8). I never want to back off from doing something because it looks too hard or because I don't want to "fail." That is to say, Jesus helps us in our Christian walk, and He's always there to pick us up should we fall.

Baptism means death. It means, "Hello! Ready for a fight? Ready to face temptations that blitz you daily? Ready to be a Christian in a non-Christian world? Ready to love your neighbor as you love yourself? Ready to exercise love, joy, peace, patience, kindness, goodness, faithfulness, gentleness, and self-control — the marks of a true Christian?" No one is ever ready to do that. But you have to start somewhere. You get saved, you get wet. Baptism is your public pledge of total and complete allegiance to your Lord and Master and Savior and Redeemer and Best Friend. And as a Spirit-filled Christian, you should be able to keep on running your race to the glory of God.

17

MY PHILOSOPHY OF RUNNING

Greek scholar Ray van Neste once asked, "Why don't more of our Greek students use what they learned in seminary?" He made a statement I will never forget:

Whether it's exercise or whether it's the study of something else, you've got to get it into the regular rhythm of life.

There you have it. That's it. Greek teaching made simple. Loving what I do — absolutely *loving* what I do — has made the world of difference for me. I've heard it said that less than one percent of the American public will ever run and compete in a full marathon. But the thing is, any reasonably healthy person can do this. Of course, everyone is *not* doing it. I am doing it because I *want* to do it and I *can* do it.

I've come to realize that taking care of my temple is not optional for me as a follower of Jesus. Having big goals and races to train for are now a part of my life. Folks, you can choose to exercise, or you can choose to be a couch potato. Or, applied to the study of Greek, *if you love the Greek language, you will use it.* And you will only get "better and stronger" for the effort. Loving what you do will make a world of difference. The feeling of mastery of Greek is like nothing else. If you keep up your motivation, you'll be unstoppable. Guaranteed. Take a lesson from my philosophy of running:

1) *Take one day at a time.* Rome wasn't built in a day. And training has to be regular and consistent. Ditto for language study.

2) *Remember: I am an athlete.* Some days I love getting out there and running, and some days I have to force myself to run. Either way, I AM A RUNNER. I won't quit. I won't stop. I won't let up. Ditto for studying Greek.

3) *Never regret a day of running.* Not one. Exercise is something I'm going to do until I'm too old and decrepit to get out of bed. The demands are huge but so are the benefits. I *love* my new life and will never go back to the goal-less, unmotivated person I was several years ago. Ditto for Greek. Either *you are a Greek student* or *you are not.* If you are one, you know you will never go back to your life before you learned Greek.

4) *Be thankful.* Thank You, Lord, for the beautiful creation I get to enjoy each and every day. Thank You for providing me with shoes that fit my feet. Thank You for race day excitement. Thank You for making me thinner and healthier. Thank You for inspiring me to be all I can be. Thank You for helping me achieve new dreams and reach new goals. *Thank You.* And to all my Greek students, past, present and future, I say: May your Greek "shoelaces" stay tied, may you make "exercise" (in your Greek studies) a regular part of your life, and may your heart always be your guide.

18

A QUEST FOR MEANING

"Quest."
A long or arduous search for something, usually
involving an adventurous journey.

I haven't met a mortal who isn't on some kind of quest for meaning in their life. What's your quest? What's mine?

Action is always compelled by some good we want to attain. The question is: Which good? And: Shall I aim for the immediate good at hand, or for a higher, better good in the future? Am I willing to deny myself the desire to enjoy life this very minute, or am I willing to deny immediate gratification for higher goals?

A marathon is a good example. It's evident that millions of Americans are training for marathons because they are convinced it's good for them to do so. Nevertheless, the tendency is to backslide and return to habits that marked our pre-marathon lives. We lack motivation. Motivation is the desire to act in a certain way to achieve a certain end. If drives push us, motivations pull us. I would like to write a book. I would like to climb a mountain. I would like to surf a big wave. I would to have a better relationship with that person. I would like to love others sacrificially. All of us have desires. The problem is that motivation is not the same thing as the dedication and sacrifice needed to get what we want.

The last time I watched the movie *Spirit of the Marathon*, I was reminded that there are no formulas for successfully completing a 26.2 mile race. There is no "rule book" out there that tells you everything you have to do and all the things you have to avoid. You have to be, well, *you*. I will never win a race. I will never receive the Nobel Prize for literature. I will never climb Everest. There are other people who know more, do more, and accomplish more than I do. But I am not them. I am my own performance. I become my latest book. I become the mountain I climb. I become the wave I ride. I become the relationship I want. I become the sacrificial person I want to be. These are all part of me.

Everything in my life changed when I decided to train for a race. My goal went from being healthy and taking care of my temple to being able to complete a 5K or a 10K or a half or full marathon. Every time I lace up my shoes I know what my goal is, what my objectives are. When in life we move into training mode — for whatever goal you might have, from being a good parent to completing a novel — we accept the risk of knowing that we will have to test our limits from time to time. There's a fine edge between doing too much to accomplish our goals and doing just enough. You just accept whatever God-given talent you have and then go out and see what happens.

Trying is everything. That's true whether your goal is to survive the loss of a spouse or get a promotion at work. For me, running has shortened the distance between what I am and what I want to become. It's my quest for meaning in life, but it's also a sport by which I can learn to play the life game better. I have come to realize that my life — like yours — is extraordinary in every way. Like you, as I pursue my goals I have to adjust to new stresses, new strengths, and new weaknesses. And I have to do so while staying focused on the real goal: finishing the race of life.

Since Becky died, I've learned that life is more about tenacity than talent. I don't have to be a professional athlete to accomplish great things. Even an unknown 12-minute miler like me can bask in the glory of race-day success, even if I come in last. Running makes us athletes in all areas of life because it trains us in the basics of living.

So that's it — the *why* of my running. I run because it is who I am — no less than the creation of the person I am meant to be. How about you?

19

THE PRIZE
IS THE JOURNEY

I think I love spring mainly because it's a reminder that God is granting His creation new life, new colors, and eventually a new Eden. It's also a reminder that nothing about my life is perfect. Like all of creation, I'm a-moanin' and a-groanin' for the ultimate Day of Redemption. I wish I could say that everything about my running life was perfect. But life is rarely perfect. I sometimes worry about minor aches and pains that I experience. Though I'm still able to walk normally and could probably run, when my body tells me to slow down I have to take it easy for a few days and refrain from running. The angst of not being able to run worries me.

The sport of running can be become addicting. Since I started running I've felt so good about myself. The joy of racing is like no other. Running is now a part of my daily life, as much as teaching is, or writing. I run because I enjoy it. Running has offered me rewards beyond my expectations. If you run long enough you'll run across some really phenomenal people, people who will inspire you, people who will remind you that all of us have a God-given ability to overcome so much. If you've ever gone through something really hard, you can appreciate what running can do for your spirit. So much of running is like life. By running we push against all the No's that try to trap us into apathy.

The human being is wired with a desire to strive for something bigger than themselves. When I do a 5K instead of sleeping in, I feel like a superhero. Running has taught me that I can persevere in the race of life. I become a more balanced and responsible version of myself. The crazy adventures I've had while training and racing definitely satisfy a craving in my soul that is vastly different from the world one sees only through a computer screen. As cliché as it sounds, I know running plays a role in my ability to work harder as a teacher and scholar. It helps me set goals in other areas of my life. As my son-in-law once told me, signing up for a race forces you to prepare for it. The finish line is nice, but the prize is in the journey.

The fun, the excitement, the comradery, the promise of a good story to tell later on — all these are reasons why I keep doing races. Running has taught me what I'm capable of. Of course, it's also given me ugly toes and aches and pains. So when my body tells me to rest up, I'll listen and see what the Lord has in store for me. I appreciate everything running has taught me, even if it's a lesson in patience.

20

BEING THERE
FOR EACH OTHER

I read a story recently, written by a serious runner, in which he admitted he wouldn't run a race if it didn't support a good cause. I'm with you, bro! The people you meet at an event are people you may never see again in your lifetime. But for this one time — for these few minutes — we can scream our hearts out for each other and help those who are facing difficulties go further. We aren't only cheering them in their race of life but squeezing our encouragement into them for whatever they might be facing next. After all, we are all running our own races in life and need all the encouragement we can get.

Recently another runner passed me toward the end of a race and both of us attempted to smile at each other but physically we couldn't. The best we could manage was a head nod in acknowledgement of the other's existence. Life is like that at times. All you can manage is an audible grunting noise. But you keep on going. You have to. I've heard runners say, "Fake it till you make it," meaning if you act like a runner long enough you might just eventually become one. And the best part of the sport is that we can be there for each other.

21

MAKE THE MOST OF TIME

Read Ephesians 5 and you will be blown away by Markus Barth's commentary. When Paul writes, "Redeeming the time, because the days are evil," he doesn't clearly state what he means. "Not even the means to be employed or the price to be paid for the redemption of time is mentioned," writes Barth. "Only one thing is clear: the transitoriness, deceptiveness, and adversity of the time in which the saints live does not excuse the people of God from using every opportunity and tackling each task they are given" (pp. 578-579).

I keep thinking about the bodies God has given us. We take care of them — hopefully, good care of them. And why? Because God gave us these bodies, and we value them. But as certainly as He created us in His image, He also created the earth. So why do we fear "creation care"? And what about our work? Clearly, labor is important to God. And did I mention rest? Not only do I not take rest all that seriously, I act like it's not even in the Bible. No, I'm not a sabbatarian, but sheesh — I need to learn how to stop filling my calendar with so many activities that I feel exhausted.

Honestly, I need to get a lot better about redeeming the time. I think the solution is just simple moment-by-moment communion with God — a natural kind of relationship between two people who spend a lot of time together. I serve a Savior who finds a way to remind me that my decisions about "time" matter to Him. This is why walking in the Spirit is so crucial.

22

EVERY PART
IS IMPORTANT

In any given race, about 5 percent of the runners are "elite" runners. The other 95 percent are not. But they are no less runners for that reason. Ironically, the people who garner the most attention are the few favored runners who are doing only 5 percent of the work. Likewise, in our churches, it's easy to develop a leader-centric paradigm in which discipleship is staff-driven. The result is a consumer culture where people think that their growth is ultimately dependent on Sunday morning sermons and Thursday evening discipleship groups. Intentional or not, the result is a church subculture in which spirituality is measured by church attendance and program allegiance. I am suggesting, not a lessened emphasis on qualified leaders in our churches, but a renewed emphasis on every member ministry wherein spiritual responsibility is transferred from leaders to Christ-followers.

How can pastors help? By enabling and equipping. By celebrating "ordinary" Christians from their pulpits. By beating the drum for simple virtues like humility, prayer, faithfulness, and sacrifice. In the Boston Marathon, as many as 8,000 volunteers assist the 35,000 runners to achieve their personal goals. Every person at the race counts.

It should be the same in our churches. We rightly place grave responsibility on our pastors. They will answer to God for their care of souls. But I wonder what would happen if we placed more expectations on the great majority of us — mere men and women of God who have the same 24 hours in which to serve King Jesus? In the early church, every person pulled their weight. Just read Acts

2. Each person was capable of a Spirit-filled life on mission with Jesus. For them, the kingdom was simple: Love God, love others. When church members are not given responsibility, they do not grow in ministry. On the other hand, when we entrust ministry to "lay" people and grant them plenty of scope for initiative, you get a church that begins to function as Paul describes in Ephesians 4 and 1 Corinthians 12. Of course, things will look less "professional" than if the pastor did all the work. But if everyone in the congregation realizes they are parts of the body, with their own special gifting, I think the whole church would begin to function in ways we can't even imagine.

Fellow "lay" person: You have so much to offer. You can raise kids who love God and serve others. You can model faithfulness to the next generation. You can open your Bible and lead a friend to Christ. You can preach peace to the poor. You can teach and admonish. You can serve in a soup kitchen. You can do the "little" things that in the kingdom are never truly little. You are gifted, endued with power from on High, so loved, so permitted. Even if others make you feel invisible, God knows and sees.

Embrace your gifts and callings. Serve the Lord with gladness. For great is your reward in heaven.

23

GET
MOVING!

Moving is not easy for any of us. Yet we all know that physical energy is necessary for anything we plan on doing in our daily lives. "Moving" develops that energy. It produces fitness of muscle, but it also produces another kind of fitness, a fitness beyond that. I'd describe it as a readiness to pursue whatever the Lord brings into our lives. Running makes people athletes in every area of their lives. They are ready for whatever comes. Like a race we do with our legs, life is made in doing and suffering and creating. All of these elements are present in a marathon race: courage, determination, discipline, will power. It creates what Maslov might describe as "peak performance."

Running can trigger that. There's no word in English that can describe what it feels like to cross the finish line. Some might call it a "runner's high." For a brief moment, I am the only one crossing that finish line. I am the only one being cheered on by the crowds. The ground may have been below my feet, but heaven is above my head. Despite the warm sweat and the aching muscles, I am reborn and renewed in my soul.

The fact is that we humans are whole beings: body, soul, and spirit. The concept of "lifestyle" therefore includes our physical, mental, and spiritual selves. The race is for me what the mountain is to the climber. It's a contest in which I go out and do battle with myself. Maybe you're not into running. No problem. Go with whatever works for you. Be sure to make it fun. But wherever you are in life, take some physical exercise. In other words:

Move!

24

Run
Your Race

Believe it or not, this runner grapples with the "theology of racing" all the time. Turns out that a marathon can teach you tons about real life and how to face the obstacles the evil one throws at you. Face it: Hebrews 12:1-2 has a lot more to do with living the Christian life than running an actual foot race. When I run my next race, it will be like any other foot race I've done. Places will change. Paces will vary. I'll run next to somebody for a while and then someone else will take his or her place. We are, after all, instant kin. Off we'll go, sharing the same feelings and fears, joys and woes, successes and failures. Non-verbal communication will bind us together. But in the end, each one of us runs our own race. Nobody can run it for us.

Let's go over Hebrews' "list of things to do" again:

☐ Draw encouragement from our fellow runners.

☐ Rid ourselves of every little thing that would slow us down.

☐ Determination is crucial, so don't leave that behind when the gun goes off.

☐ Focus on the finish line.

I see life as a gift, and every race becomes a lesson in living that I'll never forget. I will make progress toward the perfection that always seems beyond our reach, filled with zeal, fired with enthusiasm. To get to the finish will take everything I have, and more. If I do finish the race, it won't matter if I come in 3,000th or 30,000th. Winning doesn't matter. It's the *running* that counts.

If anyone makes you feel like you'll never be able to finish the race of life, write a new narrative in your heart. Run *your* race. You don't have to be fast, just determined. Will you make it? You will. We will. Together.

25

VOLUNTEERISM

No marathon would be possible without a vast array of volunteers. Think: information booth (who? what? where?), gear check (pre- and post-race), corral ("chute 'em!"), aid station (hydration support), cheer station (cheer, laugh, scream), course entertainment (are you an Elvis impersonator?), post-race area (hand out medals, distribute food and water), tear-down crew (which, well, tears everything down). When I run, I see these volunteers everywhere. They literally keep me going. Even runners are "volunteers" in the sense that we pay our own way to run, and many of us are running for a charitable cause of one kind or another.

If you want to see a good picture of a what New Testament "deacon" should look like, look no further. Deacons are servers, plain and simple. And get this: We are all to be serving one another, whether or not we have the title "deacon." I say this because many churches today have two categories of people: the ordained, and the ordinary. But there's good news. More and more I'm seeing in my students a willingness to challenge this way of thinking. In fact, today God is ordaining the ordinary. Shepherds (pastors) gladly see themselves first and foremost as fellow sheep. There is a great deal of New Testament teaching about spiritual gifts, about serving one another in love. Every single writer mentions its gravity. Fellow-service — isn't this part and parcel of our salvation? Then why isn't it a reality for so many? What happened to the spirit of volunteerism?

May the world see in us committed family members who can't get enough of each other, members of a body that requires a thousand moving parts to function optimally. We are capable of that kind of Spirit-filled life without constant management by our leaders. The tools for kingdom service are ours for the asking: the Bible, willing hands, and a heart full of Jesus.

26

REWARDS BEYOND OUR EXPECTATIONS

Sometimes I think, "What would I be like today had I never gotten into running?" Oddly, and despite my innate laziness, this sport didn't end up like so many other 21-day fads, adopted and then abandoned. What makes running so wonderful for some of us is that from our very first step we *got* it. Running met our need for courage and conviction. It helped us to move off the spot we seemed to be stuck in. Every step takes us closer to who we want to be.

I think of every race as a pure gift from God. Each day that I can get out of bed and exercise is a day I can treasure. I guess you could say I'm living life literally one step at a time. At my age, I realize that nothing lasts forever. At the same time, life ain't over till it's over, and we humans need to keep growing and striving and improving. Running has taught me that there is joy in accepting the infirmities of old age, as long as I'm always discovering new secrets about myself. Every run opens some window into my soul. Running has taught me that I can persevere. It's taught me self-discipline. In fact, when you become disciplined in one area of your life, that discipline tends to spill over into other areas of your life as well.

Something inside of us humans needs a finish line, a symbolic "game plan." What's more, we need to fight for something bigger than ourselves. Charity and good works fill a void inside us that just sitting behind a desk all day can't. As in the church, there's a solidarity in the running community. I once spoke to a high school student who told me he'd like to get involved in running. I told him about one group that has sponsored races — the Richmond Road Racers Club. I've spoken with a number of the club's members. Their support goes far beyond running. How about you? You may not be the fastest runner or even the most dedicated person out there but running will embrace you anyway and offer you rewards beyond your expectations. As I face the challenge of growing older, of ever-changing relationships, of all the good and bad that life brings, I realize that I'll have to dig deep. And I can because through Christ I have a mighty reserve of strength.

27

FAITH IS MORE THAN WHAT WE DO IN A BUILDING

Racing has become a classroom for me. I'm learning my limitations — and maybe even my potential. I am literally running for my life. If my kids bury me early, it won't because I was out of shape. There is something noble about an assembly of people knocking themselves out for the sake of a cheap finisher's medallion. The rules of racing are simple: Get to the starting line and do your dead-level best to finish.

I especially love running for good causes. There is nothing triumphalistic about this approach. Nothing arrogant. It has a simple authenticity that comes from suffering, from showing compassion to the poor, and from the generosity and involvement of donors from all the over the developed world. One of my favorite sayings is by Dorothy Day: "Don't call us saints; we don't want to be dismissed that easily."

As Christians, our lips can't proclaim one message and our lives another. These are humbling reflections. We are far too prone to see Christianity as something we do in a church building. It is far more than that. Giving of our time and energy for a cause like this takes us to the very heart of God. Magnetized by God's great gift (2 Corinthians 9:15), Christian runners joyfully do what little they can. Praise God for believers with generous hearts. The glory goes to Him. And we get the joy of honestly sharing the Gospel with others both in deed and in word.

28

JOINING JESUS
AT THE BOTTOM

Did you know that students at the College of Charleston can take a class called Sport Physiology and Marathon Training? Bet you'll never guess what the final exam is. You guessed *exactly* right. Running a marathon. I ask you humbly: How can students take a class on the New Testament at seminary and remain overfed, arrogant, and unconcerned? The U.S. spends more on trash bags than almost half the world spends on all goods combined. This helps me better understand Paul's teaching in 1 Timothy 1:5: "The goal of our instruction is love." I like how *The Message* puts it: "The whole point of what we're urging is simply *love* — love uncontaminated by self-interest and counterfeit faith, a life open to God."

I'm finally beginning to connect the dots. An old Scottish proverb puts it this way: "Greek, Hebrew, and Latin have their proper place, but it's not at the head of the cross where Pilate put them, but at the foot of the cross in humble service to Jesus." God is requiring obedience from our New Testament students. Not the kind that is little more than an hour of inconvenience on Sunday morning. The next time there's a *Run for Nepal* — a 5K race in Morrisville, NC dedicated to raising funds to rebuild that country after its devastating 2013 earthquake — I hope hundreds of born-again Jesus freaks will sign up with me. "Broken and poured out for you" is the way Jesus, I think, would put it. Jesus left heaven to come to the foulest place in the universe only to be betrayed by His own. When His followers are asked to do the same thing, they can only hear and obey.

Richard Rohr writes that "... power, prestige, and possessions are the three things that prevent us from recognizing the reign of God...." (*Simplicity,* p. 56). The pattern of ascent is so ingrained in our circles that it may be physically painful for some of us to reject it. But if we are to "take the lowest place" (Luke 14:10), we'll need to get off our high horses.

I hate this kind of simplicity. I hate being asked to be countercultural, even as an academic. But that's where I am, folks. I am so over upward mobility. I'm ready to join to Jesus at the bottom. And to ask you to do the same.

29

STEWARD WELL

It's only by the grace of God that I get to do *anything*. "What do you have that wasn't given to you? Answer that! So, if you've really received it all as a sheer gift, why take the credit to yourself?" That's God's word on the matter. My taking credit for being able to run is as absurd as my taking credit for my salvation. Not only the gift of running has been given to me, but the very air I breathe while I'm running has. "All good giving, as well as every perfect gift, comes from above, from the Father." Just because God gives us things indirectly (such as the ability to work out or train or lift weights), that's no reason to forget that He's still the one giving it to us. Jesus said, "Beware of greed of every kind! Don't be like the man whose crops yielded so much that he pulled down his old barns and built bigger ones, then said to himself, 'Look at what *I've* done! Time to take life easy, eat, drink, and enjoy yourself, Dave old buddy old pal.'" You guys, this is *exactly* me from time to time. I'm learning, ever so slowly, to give God the credit. The one who is reluctant to acknowledge that God is the giver of all his gifts is the one who will also be reluctant to part from them. And one day we must all "part from them." Health and vitality will be gone. God may even take our possessions from us. Okay. What then? Here's Paul's answer:

I count all these things as unspeakable filth for the sake of gaining Christ and finding myself united with Him. All I really care about is to know Christ and to be conformed to His death.

Alright. I'm not there. Still, I truly believe that life and light are greater than darkness. I also believe that humility is no excuse for being anything less than God wants us to be. Clothes, food, health, money, houses, vacations, family: all are pure gifts from His hand. "All these things the heathen run after, but not you. Your heavenly Father knows you need all of them." God is the Giver. I am the steward. That's about it. If we truly get this right, I believe everything else will fall into place.

30

ATHLETES
FOR JESUS

Within the framework of Philippians, 3:12-18 holds a special place in my heart. After all, here Paul uses a running analogy. Throughout Paul's writings we see people running races. Paul calls the church — men and women — to be athletes for Jesus. Knowing Christ (Philippians 3:1-11) involves a daily discipline of pressing toward the goal (3:12-18). Even Paul hasn't arrived yet. He's still running his race, pursuing Christ with everything he's got. He describes this as "straining on toward what's ahead." Yep. Paul must have been a distance runner. I'm still learning from him what it means to run the race of faith. I'm learning not to avoid the race or complain about it. Let me pass on a few other lessons as well:

1) *Learn to set reasonable and achievable goals.* This is one of the most difficult things for runners to do. But it's one of the most important lessons running teaches us. Realize that your running goals are just that — *your* goals and not somebody else's. Paul had his goals. You have yours. I have mine. Be sure each goal is based on some standard. For Paul, that standard was attaining Christ. Of course, we don't arrive at that goal all at once. The best goals are those that allow us to build a pattern of success. Remember: A goal is simply something to aim for. It's something to be dedicated to. It's a process as much as it's an end.

2) *Listen to your body more than you listen to your well-meaning friends.* Every runner needs to make their own decisions, including the decision to accept their limitations. It felt so good when I

broke the 30-minute barrier for the first time during a 5K race. It had taken numerous attempts. I've broken 30 minutes only twice since then. Looking back, I realize now that I'm not a 30-minute 5Ker. If I really wanted to run sub-30 every time I raced, I'd run myself into the ground. "Know yourself," said the ancients. By any standard, the apostle Paul was way out ahead of most of us when it came to knowing Christ. But I'm not running against Paul; I'm running with him.

3) *Be patient with yourself.* Especially when you're tempted to look back — either to wallow in self-pity or to rest on the laurels of past achievements. Faith is not a past reality. It's a present requirement. Don't rush the process. Accept setbacks as they come. I've met runners who think they can go from a 5K to a marathon within a few months. The result is either burnout or injury. We gradually build up our endurance.

4) *Our future is in our own hands (or feet, to use Paul's metaphor).* But it's also in *God's* hands. Paul chose a goal that is utterly unattainable in its entirety and perfection. "To know Christ and the power of His resurrection and the fellowship of His sufferings — I can never do *that!*" No, I can't. At least not in my own strength. But, through the One who empowers me, I can know Christ better every day. I can experience increasingly the power of His resurrection. I can enter more and more into the fellowship of His sufferings. In other words, we arrive and keep on arriving. It's a more-than satisfying pursuit, even though we never reach it completely down here.

Friend, don't spend time in the library trying to work out a theory of running the Christian race. You have the Bible and you have Jesus. These two always agree. Bring your needs to Him with all the simplicity of a little child, for He is accessible day or night. You are always welcome. He has no favorite racers. He will coach you to the end of your journey.

31
PRACTICE
COURAGE

Even after all these years of running, races still intimidate me. Mostly because I'm not super-fast, but also because I'm still such a newbie at this whole sport. I'm not proud to admit it, but I'm pretty much a wimp when it comes to suffering, especially knowing that I could be at home in my warm slippers.

That said, it feels undeniably good to stand there at the starting line waiting for the horn to sound, knowing that my former self would definitely not have chosen to be there on race day. Then, after the race starts, I'm amazed at the willpower of my fellow sufferers: people in wheelchairs, people who have a prosthesis, people who are blind and running with a guide. How can they do that? Instead of having a pity party ("Why me?"), they ask, "Okay, so I've got issues. What new possibilities can I strive for?"

That's the great thing about racing. For this one race, for this one time, we can scream our hearts out and encourage each other. We're not only cheering for others but for ourselves. If that doesn't fire you up, your wood's all wet. Some of you need to stop "adulting" all the time. You need to try something new and jump in without knowing or worrying about the how part later. Running is like a caramel macchiato at Starbucks. It'll keep you coming back for more, and more.

Nothing inspires me more than people who risk feeling vulnerable by trying something new. I'm inspired by everyone who is brave with their lives so that others can be brave with theirs. Life is not the path of least resistance. My friend, what is the "new" God is calling you today? To practice courage is to look at life and say, "I'm all in."

Get deliberate.

Get inspired.

Get going.

32

BE THE
ENCOURAGEMENT
SOMEONE NEEDS

Watching the movie *Everest* was an eye-opener for me. The film provided an unparalleled example of leadership — or, better, lack of leadership. Neither Rob Hall nor Scott Fischer had any business climbing past their agreed-upon turnaround times. There would have been no 1996 Everest disaster had all the climbers turned around by 2:00 pm. At the South Summit, the decision by John Taske, Stuart Hutchinson, and Lou Kasischke to turn around literally saved their lives. The fact is, if both teams had followed their own safety rules, nobody would have perished. The rivalry between Hall and Fischer only added to a situation in which the leaders were already making suboptimal decisions.

The lesson here?
Sometimes life is all about saying no.

John Lennon once famously said, "Life is about what happens when you're busy making other plans." Life is a collection of thousands and thousands of little choices. But strung together through all of these little decisions, like beads on a string, is the foundation on which you're building your life. For me, this foundation is very clearly stated in Colossians 3:16, which might well function as a life verse for me. "Christ's message in all its fullness must live in your hearts. Teach and instruct one another with all wisdom." I want every student who has a class with me to go away thinking, "This class was more about Christ than about anything else." This is a "must," says Paul. Christ's message *has to* live in our hearts. It's not an option. The verb here is in the mood of command — the imperative mood. Translating it as "Let Christ's message live in your hearts" is much too bland. It makes it sound like Paul is making a suggestion. "If you want to, let it happen." Nope. It's *got to happen.* But how does it happen? That's the rest of the verse: as we "teach and instruct one another with all wisdom." This is it. *We help each other to grow into Christ.*

As I continue to run, I am amazed at just how much a "community" this running thingy is. Now that running is an integral part of my life, I draw more and more insights from the sport into my essential self. These insights are perhaps less dramatic than those I find in the Bible, but they are no less profound. Running has taught me, and continues to teach me, that there is joy in watching others succeed and in helping them make progress, just as they are willing and able to help me succeed and make progress.

This truth came home to me when I recently opened the *New York Times*. (The online edition, of course. Do people still read newspapers?) The essay was called "How the 'Shalane Flanagan Effect' Works." Remember how Shalane won the New York City Marathon? She was the first American woman to win New York in 40 years. Here's the money quote from the essay:

> But perhaps Flanagan's bigger accomplishment lies in nurturing and promoting the rising talent around her, a rare quality in the cutthroat world of elite sports. Every single one of her training partners — 11 women in total — has made it to the Olympics while training with her, an extraordinary feat. Call it the Shalane Effect: You serve as a rocket booster for the careers of the women who work alongside you, while catapulting forward yourself.

You serve as a rocket booster for those who work alongside you.

Bingo!

Flanagan discovered that the more she pushed her younger colleagues to improve, the more they pushed *her* to improve. That's what makes running such a great sport. The glory belongs not only to those runners at the front of the pack. It belongs to all of us, regardless of whether we've ever stood on the awards podium. In other words, if you run your best, you can be *beaten* but you can never be *defeated*. The struggles you have are the same struggles that everyone else has too. That's one of the greatest lessons I've learned in life.

Being a runner has made me a more naturally caring person. I discovered that the running community is made up of everyday people who are all willing to help me. You see, what binds us together as runners is far more powerful than what separates us. Shalane Flanagan understood this. She knew that there was no better way for her to become a better runner than by enabling others to become better runners themselves.

So Paul says, "Christ's message *has to* settle down and make its home in our hearts." And the way this happens is when we "teach and instruct one another with all wisdom." I don't want or need to be the teacher all the time. I want and need to be taught. I believe that if we as Christians cultivate a spirit of true fraternal instruction (as is taught in Hebrews 8), we will find the effort more than worth it. I love and respect pastors immensely. But some of the responsibilities they try to care for are well beyond their capacity. Little wonder they grow weary in trying to keep all the plates spinning. I suggest this: Develop a church culture in which discipleship is measured not by attendance but by participation. Decide, dear pastor friend, if you want to produce disciples or consumers. It was never God's intent that pastors should bear all the weight of responsibility for the spiritual growth of their flocks. Prepare your people to shepherd. Delegate more. Grant opportunities for teaching and instructing. If you haven't read it yet, grab a copy of the book *With: A Practical Guide to Informal Mentoring and Intentional Disciple Making*. The authors write:

*The younger generation desperately seeks mentors
to show them how to live for Jesus in a real world.*

Yes, I realize that "discipleship" is a buzzword today. It's all the fad. But it's actually been around for millennia. Jesus "just happened" to believe in it Himself.

Thank You, God, for the blessing of community. I thank You, as a runner, that You introduced me to a group of people who truly care about each other. Thank You for teaching me, both through the running community and through Your body, the church, that being part of something great is better than being great. Help all of us, as Paul constantly teaches us, to work together as a team for the sake of the Gospel. Help us to realize that we are both players and cheerleaders. It shouldn't be any other way.

33

TAKE TIME
TO ENJOY
WHERE YOU ARE

Each race is its own reward. Every race frees you just a little bit more from being sedentary. As an adult-onset athlete, I don't expect to be a young man again. A victory at this stage of life mostly means getting to the starting line. Trophies and medals don't matter. It's all about finding that un-tapped, God-given source of energy within yourself. I've never won a single race I've competed in, but I've been victorious dozens of times, even if I came in 23,478th place. Running can teach us to live with the dramatic shifts in our lives. Despite the hardships, running allows you to experience moments of unspeakable joy. Those moments of joy will stay with you forever.

Right now, looking back at my experiences as a runner, I know I'm not satisfied with my accomplishments. But rather than thinking only about what's left to be done, today is a day for honoring them and being grateful for what the Lord has allowed me to accomplish. I hope you will do the same. Reject the obsession with what you wish you were. Instead, focus on who you are and what you are becoming in Christ. Enjoy every moment of your accomplishment. For just a day, stop trying to get somewhere else. The joy is in knowing that just as God has led you to this point, so He will continue to lead you as you write the next chapter of your life. Being a Christian isn't simply a goal or a destination. It's a way of living life. Consistency is what it's all about. Runners know this well. Getting out there consistently, even if it's just for 15 minutes every other day, goes a long way. Consistency simply means not giving up and not giving in. I may not be able to run as far or as fast as I would like to, but that's okay because in the end what matters is the process of running, not the destination. Even today, I'm amused at all the things I've become — triathlete, mountaineer, marathoner — all because I decided to begin moving my body with my own two feet. I'm sure I'm a better person today because I'm a widower than I would have been otherwise. The answer to our loneliness is not found in another person but in surrendering to the One who loves us with an everlasting love. Once we learn to love Him with all of our hearts, He will pour out His love to others *through us.*

Dear Reader, "May the Lord satisfy your needs and cause your light to rise like dawn out of darkness. May He give you strength of limb. May He cause you to be like a well-watered garden, like a spring whose waters never fail" (Isaiah 58:9-11). May you always move in the direction of God's will.

34
ANYONE CAN
RUN A MARATHON

I once read a piece in the *New York Times* that made me scratch my head. It's called "Plodders Have a Place, But Is It in a Marathon?" One "hard core" runner who was interviewed said:

> *It's a joke to run a marathon and walk every
> other mile or by finishing in six, seven, eight hours.*

Hmm. Just a bit censorious maybe? What do you say to this guy?

First of all, to the elitist runners who complain about us penguins "walking every other mile," I want you to know that I have actually managed to walk *two miles* during a marathon. So there. Second, who am I to say how fast you should run your marathon? You see, unlike football or basketball, what makes running such a unique sport is that both first-timers and elite runners compete on the very same playing field. In the third place, there's a huge difference between pace and effort. I really don't care what anybody's pace is as long as they are pushing themselves to accomplish their personal goals. Finally, there's no one "correct" way of doing anything in life. Where I work, all of us Greek teachers use different beginning grammars. Our teaching styles are also radically different. *Vive la différence!* As long as we get the job done, we're good to go.

The bottom line? Once you cross that finish line at the marathon, you become a marathoner. Period. The elite runner's goal might be to win the race. My goal might be to get to the next mile marker without dropping dead. As far as I'm concerned, we've both accomplished something monumental. I will never be more than a very average recreational runner. I run for the fun of it and because I enjoy a good challenge. I've seen mortals of every age, size, and shape cross the finish line. I'm one of them. I'm racing the clock just like everyone else is, and I'm right proud of it. I've read that some runners who were once 3:30 finishers now take 6 hours to finish a marathon. Eventually that will happen to all of us. It's called *aging*. We can all be grateful for the gift of running. As long as we train hard and respect the distance, I think the sport is big enough to embrace us all.

35

THIS IS A GOD THING

I have grown to love the outdoors, to enjoy being active again on a regular basis. I love the fitness community. It's what I know. God has always made the most sense to me through His word and through the world that He created. I crave health and well-being for me and mine and for you and yours. But believe me, this is a God thing. I am from Hawaii, remember? I'm naturally prone to hanging loose, *bruddah.* When I see that I traveled 817 miles in one year of exercise I think, "That's not me. Good grief — that's the distance from Washington, DC to Tampa, Florida." I hope you get a laugh out of that. After all, if God can do this for a lazy kid from Kailua like me, He can do it for just about anybody I suppose. He's good at being God. That first 5K unleashed a chain reaction of liberation from being a couch potato. But God made it all possible.

This is my point: Good health is a gift from God. Pure and simple. Sure, we think we can engineer a carefully sculptured bod. I declare this is nonsense. If we are in good shape, super. But all the praise goes to Jesus. One day I'll go off the rails health-wise. We all will. Through sickness. Cancer maybe. Who knows. Maybe I'll get injured doing something stupid (er, audacious) like climbing the Alps. Friend, if you are doing your best to maintain the temple, that's good enough. We don't live in a reality TV show; we're living real lives. I'm just grateful for all the good things I've experienced being outdoors and doing silly things like running in races or hiking up hillsides.

For me, getting in shape was like completing a doctoral program. I absolutely understand why people find other things to do with their time. Yet I think that sometimes we very much under-estimate the power of God to change us. I bet we are tougher than we think. Like all human beings, we grow through struggle, failure, and perseverance. And if it turns out we never really do lose all that unwanted weight? We can still love God and follow Him. Because when our physical health tanks (and it will), He will hold us fast.

36

RUNNING IS
A VACATION

"They seek for themselves," wrote Marcus Aurelius Antoninus, "a house in the country, seashore, and the mountains. But this is altogether the mark of the common man, for it is in thy power whenever you shall choose to retire within thyself." When I run a 5K, for a brief 30 minutes, I have the freedom just to be me, without censure or praise. I am, for those 30-some-odd minutes, my own new Adam, the only one in my universe. The person that I am is expressed in the race and, when I run, my entire personality participates. Moreover, as I run, the sights and sounds, pains and pleasures of life, become available to me in a unique way. Exercise should not be looked at as a game plan for successful living. It *is* successful living.

Words fail to describe what the outdoors does to me. Exercise takes me away from my disturbed circumference to the center of my being. Almost always, the complete experience becomes timeless, selfless, beyond history or anxiety — I could almost say a "mystical" experience. Health is not the product of this activity but a process — an ongoing, continual, continuous *state of becoming* self-disciplined. It's largely our decision whether we are healthy or unhealthy, lean or overweight — and I say this because each and every one of our habitual behaviors is adopted by personal choice. Exercise deficiency is a self-inflicted wound.

So, I find my retreat in biking, running, or even getting up hay on the farm. And folks, *anybody* can do it. All it takes is sweat.

37

FACE FEAR
WITH FAITH

We often think that brave people have no fear. The truth is that we all fear the unknown. This is where faith comes in. When things frighten us, when we face risk and uncertainty, we realize that we are on the verge of something important. As I faced the challenge of climbing the Alps in 2016, I remember thinking, "Now every moment is precious to me. My family is precious to me. My life itself means so much to me." At that moment, something had changed. A thing that was scary and horrifying had turned into a gift.

Thinking that we can find lasting joy and avoid pain in this life is a pipe dream. Loss is inevitable for all of us. In fact, the times when we really know what life is all about is when the rug has been pulled out from under our feet and we haven't got the foggiest idea where we're going to land. In that very instant of fear is the seed of hope. Life is a good teacher. As humans, we are always living in transition. But as we stay with the uncertainty — as we live with a broken heart — we will find the path of true awakening.

When things get edgy, we need to ask ourselves, "Am I going to open up or shut down?" We don't need to try and create these situations. They will present themselves to us with clockwork regularity. And when they do, we have no choice except to embrace what's happening or push back against it. Underneath our ordinary lives — underneath all the teaching I do, all the traveling I do, all that's in my mind — there is a fundamental groundlessness that can only be grounded in Christ. Christ is like the Matterhorn. A lot happens to a mountain. The rain hits it. The wind howls. It snows. Clouds cross it. People climb it. Many things happen to the mountain. But it just sits there. When we see who we are in Christ, when we refuse to find our identity in anything or anyone else, there is a grounding like a mountain.

Here's my invitation to you. Step out of denial, and deal with whatever you've been given. Approach it head on. Face down your fears. Your place in Christ is secure. And His Holy Spirit is an unbelievable healer. Give your losses to Jesus. He can do something positive with them, I tell you. You can cross the finish line. And never forget that we are running this race together.

38

RUNNING AS AN ACT OF WORSHIP

All of life comes with challenges, with ups and downs. But here's the deal. The ups and down aren't negatives. God calls us to a life of hardship and self-discipline so that we would trust Him and not ourselves. He also created each and every one of us with unique desires and goals. We have a Savior who loves us, saves us from our sins and worries and insecurities, and encourages us to embrace the challenges and races of life with joy. A race is a celebration, fueled by joy and propelled by God's strength.

I choose running and biking and surfing and climbing because they're what God has given me to use to worship Him, relate to others, and love the lost. All of these activities are so much bigger, so much grander, than sporting activities. For me it means living daily in relation with Christ and with others. And so I choose to live in celebration, to keep moving forward in life, attuning my heart to God's, pressing on to maturity. Being outdoors is how I communicate best with my Creator God. My sweet Becky isn't here to enjoy it with me, but God is using my activities to raise awareness about endometrial cancer. There *is* life after cancer, I can promise you that.

You see, being active is an act of worship. Whenever I run, I rejoice in God's strength, in His faithfulness, in His promises for all of my needs. Mentally, physically, and spiritually, I believe I have what it takes to compete in the game of life.

39
THE FATHER RUNS

A Bible verse that runners love is Isaiah 40:31: "But those who trust in the Lord will find new strength. They will soar high on wings like eagles. They will run and not grow weary. They will walk and not faint." See it? Isaiah talks about flying (I do a lot of that nowadays), running (ahem, marathoner here!), and walking (my favorite pace). Of course, Isaiah didn't mention mountain biking or surfing, but hey, you can't expect him to think of everything.

Speaking of running, I often think of that scene in the story of the Prodigal Son (Luke 15) where the father breaks out in a full sprint toward his returning son. Can you imagine how his son felt? Distinguished Middle Eastern dads normally didn't do 5Ks. Did he run to protect his son? Many think so. The boy had disgraced his father and had brought shame on the entire village. Were perhaps the elders about to intercept him and send him back to his pig sty? Can't you just see the father reaching his son and embracing him, at the same time telling the elders, "This is *my* son! I love him! If you tell him to leave, I'm leaving too!"

Wow! The world needs more dads like that.

40

THE ANCIENT WORLD

How were foot races conducted in the ancient world? Glad you asked.

- ☐ Runners (males only) ran naked. Well, there goes the Nike endorsement! Hebrews 12:1 may well refer to the "laying aside" of clothing as athletes did before competing.

- ☐ Most races were simple 200-yard (600-foot) dashes. That was pretty much the length of the stadium (hence a foot race was called a *stade*).

- ☐ The longest distance was 24 stades, or about 2.86 miles. The "marathon" was unknown at the time (it's an invention of the 1896 Olympic Games).

- ☐ Training was taken very seriously.

- ☐ "Endurance" was considered important even during shorter races. Hence the reference to endurance in Hebrews 12:1.

- ☐ Victory brought great prestige. (Think medallion and bragging rights today. And the t-shirt, of course.)

41

DIG DEEP

I know in the big scheme of things, running a foot race is not headline news, but I gotta to tell you, it forces you to dig deep. I'm eager to do another marathon, because the last one I did almost killed me. Yes, folks, runners are kinda crazy in that way. We love suffering. There is no "secret" to being a runner. To become a runner, all you have to do is, well, run. And by "run," I don't necessarily mean to literally "run." I've yet to run an entire marathon. I probably never will. Still, there's nothing quite like standing at the start of a 26.2 mile race and asking your body to do more than it's used to doing. Plus, what's not to enjoy? From improved cardiovascular fitness to better health, there's so much benefit from participating in this crazy sport.

I am proud of my finishing times, even when I'm slower than everybody else in my age group. A clock is never reflective of the kind of person you are. Great races can be had by all, even the slowest among us. You'll find that learning how to run a race is mostly about putting forth an honest effort. When it's over, the only question you to need to ask yourself is, "Did I do my best?"

The truth is that every race takes me a little bit closer to where I want to be in life. Your goals are just that — *your* goals, not somebody else's. So find something you enjoy doing, and just get out there and do it. Go ahead. Test your limits. Make no mistake: Living life to the fullest is something each one of us can do, with God's help.

42

It's Never too Late to Set Goals

What would your life be like if you said to yourself:

- ☐ No more adventures for me.

- ☐ I think I'll just take it easy from here on out.

- ☐ I am enough.

Huh?

What are your personal goals for this year? Are you meeting them? Have you given up? Yeah, I know how easy it is to overcommit. I'm pretty much an expert at that. So here's what you can do: Pick goals you are super-excited about. Two of my hard-working kids have gone back to school. They couldn't wait to text me their first day back to remind me. (Oh, they were not spring chickens either. They were just ramping up their career goals.) Another one of my daughters decided to write her very first book. And boy is she a good writer. By the way, be sure to write down your goals. That's the difference between a goal and a wish. Once I get an idea in my head, I usually write it down. I love the fact that goals need to be challenging. Am I crazy? Or just goal-oriented? Or both? Believe it not, the more I age, the more goals I set for myself. Individual goals. Family goals. Writing goals. Travel goals. I try to be realistic. People tend to overestimate what they can accomplish in a short period of time. Still, I love writing down my goals and reviewing them every so often (like about once a week, like on Monday mornings, in fact).

So have you written down your goals? Visualize exactly the person God wants you to be. Your success depends on complete dependence on Him, and then following through with His plans for you.

43

FIND
BALANCE

How do we find just that right balance between exercise and rest? For me, the porridge is usually a little too hot or too cold, when it needs to be "just right" (thank you, Goldilocks). Sometimes I ask myself, "Self, are you working out too much?" In other words, regardless of the number of miles or hours we put in monthly, the solution to the balance question is to listen to our bodies. They are usually quick to tell us when we're doing too much. When we push ourselves beyond what they are ready for, we experience fatigue and pain. It's really just that simple. That's why we have to listen to our bodies *attentively*. If we don't, we may find ourselves working too hard and thus working *against* ourselves. Again, it's all a matter of balance. I want to be a good Goldilocks.

Moreover, I'm beginning to see the relevance of training for my non-running life as well. Through running I'm hoping to find that balance in my everyday life that often eludes me. Facebook? There's only one site I read. Goodbye everyone else. TV? Haven't watched it in years (except every time I go out for dinner — where a TV is in every nook and cranny of the restaurant, even in the men's room. Yikes). I've also pressed the reset button on getting news online. Let's be honest: I don't have time to stay engaged with all the news outlets that are demanding my attention 24/7. Without the noise and static of being online, I'm learning how to rest and simplify. I know that a media fast won't make the evening news, but I gotta tell you, it's so liberating. As for emails, I'm really good at answering them quickly, perhaps too good. I like people who respond to my texts and emails immediately. But later responses don't hurt anybody. All too often I hold myself at gunpoint by the expectations of others. Let's face it, that works for only so long.

So where do things stand as of today? Few care whether or not I fast from social media. Instead, this week I hope to find quality time with family while not neglecting my workouts and my farm jobs. Maybe this is a new beginning on a new perspective on balance. Hopefully so. And hopefully you find it too.

44

WHY I RUN

Here is why I run:

1) *Praise.* Running reminds me how shockingly gracious God is, and how free we are to love Him back with all our mind, soul, strength, and bodies. Yes, with our *body*, that physical thing wrapped around me that tells me I'm in my mid-60s when I'm really only 35. It's His, all His, but it matters what we do with it.

2) *Appreciation.* For the men and women and boys and girls I see out on the course every time I lace up. Who would have known how great the running community has turned out? I've met some really amazing people from all over the nation and even the world at racing events. Now if only fewer of them over 65 would run, I might have a shot at a medal.

3) *Fitness.* Live long enough and it becomes clear that health is a pure gift of the Lord. One of the best parts of being human is taking care of the "tent" He's given us. No, we don't live and breathe for health. We live for the love of Jesus and for the love of our families and for the love of a lost world. Honestly, that's why taking care of our bodies matters.

4) *Challenge.* Every day, every week, every month there are new goals to accomplish. What a chance to really test our limits. I deeply believe that God wants this for us, that He delights in seeing us challenge ourselves with bigger and greater goals. So few of us

live up to our God-given potential. What a loss. What a tragedy. We can never get those years back again.

5) *Happiness.* Running is like a drug. I am a happier person because of activity. It helps me cope with all the "stuff" in my life.

Thank you, Running!

45

TAKE
RESPONSIBILITY

Athletes leverage stress to become better. Through training they learn that everything matters — nothing is neutral. If you put miles on your feet every week, there's a price to pay. If you study hard for an exam, you will likely get a good grade. The Greeks called this *askesis* (training) and they believed that all of us must become "athletes" in every sense of the word: physically, mentally, emotionally, and spiritually.

I believe the next breakthrough in medicine won't be due to a surgeon devising a new method of surgery. It will be the individual patient — you and I — taking responsibility for our own health. This can occur every morning in your kitchen. *"Man isst was er ist,"* say the Germans. "You are what you eat." That goes for the spiritual too. Not just what you hear from the pulpit on Sunday morning, but what you read each and every day from God's word, can produce astonishing new levels of spiritual health and fitness.

The one thing physicians are doing more today than ever before is focusing not on pathology but on the patient. One aspect of disease that I can control is my diet and level of daily exercise. I don't drink enough water every day. I need to change that. Soda is not good for me. I can cut out soft drinks. Fast food is junk food. So why give in to the convenience? Diets don't work. Then why I am trying out that new fad diet?

This is one of the things that motivates me to keep entering races. Back-of-the-packers like me are no less runners than the elite racers. Occasionally I hear runners complain that age has robbed them of their speed. I have to laugh. I'll never "look back" at my speed because I never had it. Even when I come in second to last (as I did one time at a marathon in Allen, TX, where it was 1 degree on race day and only 44 runners finished the race out of 700 registrants), I felt the enormous pleasure that comes from giving it your all. I doubt that any Roman legionnaire felt any prouder.

This happens to me every time I pin on a race number. Girded with the latest style of running shoes and Body Glide to protect those "sensitive" parts of the anatomy, you make your way to the starting line, ready to do battle. The veterans gather around and give support as you take your place at the rear echelon. Running produces fitness of muscle, but it also produces another kind of fitness, a fitness that goes way beyond the physical. Life is a game that's played on more than the physical plane. And frankly, I wouldn't want to play the game in any other way. Mind, body, and spirit — all cooperating, each showing you where you fit in the grand scheme of things.

Ultimately, when you run, you explore the limits of your whole person. We have to prepare for life in much the same way that an athlete trains for a big race. The same basic skills are involved. There are no tricks or gimmicks here. To play the game of life well, we have to be involved individually. Running helps to develop that discipline — and, of course, any other form of exercise you might prefer over running.

There is a place in life for the sedentary, like sitting at a table grading exams. But we can't go through life as though we were simply intellectual animals. The best we can do is be prepared, live each day as it comes to us, fill each hour with love, and grapple with the mystery of living.

46

CONTINUAL EXPANSION

I love the book *Running Until You're 100*, by Jeff Galloway. Here are a few quotes:

- "If exercise were a controlled medication, it would be the most heavily prescribed on record."

- "Running stimulates your body to improve overall physical and mental capacity."

- "I want you to take control of your running enjoyment and fatigue while staying injury free."

- "Unfortunately, many people over the age of 50 believe that they cannot, or should not, increase their level of exercise."

- "The evidence is growing that running and walking will bring quality to your life, increase longevity and will not harm your joints — when done correctly."

- "Older runners can improve faster than younger runners."

- "One of the fastest growing age groups in many parts of the running world is the 80+ division."

- "In many ways, running is more important to older runners."

- "Many veterans find that they run faster while covering fewer miles per week, especially fewer days per week."

- "Walk breaks let you erase fatigue and damage to the legs and body."

- "Our bodies are designed to improve through a series of challenges."

- "Stress + Rest = Improvement."

All of these things seem so obvious to me now. Just several years ago, it was all Greek to me. But life involves continual expansion. We learn to discharge what is latent within us. And each stage is an achievement.

Achieve well, my friends. When you reach a plateau, consider what you learned from that stage of life. And then unflaggingly pursue the next one with excellence.

47

DEDICATE YOURSELF TO PROGRESS

Sometimes dedication means doing what you don't want to do. The best elite runners are not only disciplined but dedicated. And that's something we can all strive for. Dedicated to your spouse. To your kids. To your studies. To exercise. To achieving a God-given goal. It's important to understand that where you start isn't as important as where you're headed. Your progress won't always conform to a strict time-table. Progress comes gradually, over time. In fact, all of life is like that — full of mystery — and it's this mystery that keeps us going. "What's around that next bend?" we ask ourselves. It might surprise you. It might even be to run in the Boston Marathon, and you, yes you, are about to finish.

Every one of us has our own race to run. Sometimes we run outside of our comfort zone. Sometimes we're sidelined. Sometimes we lose interest in the race. Then we remember what running is all about – what it's like to do hard things, to push through one more obstacle, to learn again what your body's and mind's limits are. Lord willing I hope to do a lot more running in the years to come. For me, there's no better way to achieve perspective in life. So it's — *forge ahead!* Trust the Lord for the results. Real success in life comes from being willing to take risks. We can't, therefore, settle for comfort. Just focus on what you do well and forget about "beating" anyone else. After all, there will always be people who are smarter, more productive, faster, etc. than you are. In Christ we are the Father's children, beloved and treasured, and that's good enough.

48

HARNESS YOUR
MOTIVATION

Your *mindset* is the most important thing when you run. We "get" to run, remember? It's never something we *have* to do. Running, like anything in life, is a decision. You either decide to make running a part of your life or you don't. Ditto for all things academic.

Growing up, I always admired smart people. Since I never had their cachet, I figured I could be a mediocre student in high school. But when I got to college, all of that changed. I had become a "student." Let's get real. Not everyone in school is a student. They're more interested in a degree than in learning. What makes the difference between someone who's just going through motions and someone who's committed to a lifetime of learning? It's motivation. Yes. I said it. The M-word.

Each of us is driven farther and faster when we do something we love. Harnessing the power of intrinsic motivation rather than extrinsic remuneration is thoroughly satisfying and infinitely more rewarding. Carrots and sticks (often) don't work. I say "often" because sometimes we have to use extrinsic motivation to nudge ourselves along. But an operating system centered around rewards and punishment can only do so much.

The starting point, of course, is to fall back on extrinsic motivators only when absolutely necessary. I give quizzes and exams. In Basel, that would have been unthinkable. A quiz over the reading material? Ridiculous. I'm reading the book because that's what I love to do. But here in the States, the game we play is called the tyranny of the urgent. I do only as much as I'm expected to do because

I have little to no time to do anything else. If we want to strengthen our academic institutions, get beyond our underachievement, and address the problem of mediocrity in our lives, our businesses, and our world, we need to move from Type-X behaviors (X-trinsic) to Type-I behaviors (I-ntrinsic).

Of course, none of us ever truly exhibits purely intrinsic behavior every waking moment. I know I don't. A publisher sets a deadline for my manuscript. Whether I feel like it or not, I have to meet that deadline. But in the long run, I believe that Type-I people outperform Type-X people. No, we don't disdain money or recognition. But we're motivated by something more lasting than that. For the follower of Jesus, that motivation is pleasing Him.

So we have a choice. We can cling to our old habits or craft a new approach to help ourselves work a little smarter and a little better. Getting an A in Greek is a performance goal. But being able to use Greek once you've graduated is a learning goal. Both goals can fuel achievement, but only one leads to mastery.

49

RUNNING
IS LIFE

Running is a parable for the rest of life. As with running, so with life: you have goals, you have expectations, you have failures, and you have excuses galore. Running doesn't define me, but it has helped me get through the challenges I've faced. I'm finally coming into my second adulthood (thanks Gail Sheehy!), trying to make the world a little bit kinder, better, more beautiful, wiser, and maybe even funnier. To switch to a musical metaphor, I am an orchestra musician playing my note just like you are playing yours, and together we are making fantastic music. We grin at each as we run our respective races, inspired by our mutual doggedness, realizing just how risky it is to step off on shaky legs, but we do it anyway because — well, is there any other option in life?

Wisdom is a process. It can't be rushed, just like I had to take one slow, agonizing step after the other to summit the brutal Breithorn in 2016. I think the biggest slice of humble pie I ever got was when we had to turn around on the Matterhorn because my foot was killing me (and a storm was brewing). It was a slap in the face and a much-needed one too, because I needed to learn how to respect the mountains and even more respect the training and time that goes into such things. I also learned through my mountain guide that no matter who we are we don't finish this life alone. We need each other. There is always someone to help you or cheer you on.

Nowadays it seems I can find a way to relate everything in life to either running or mountaineering. When I'm active I'm really *living*. As someone has said, if you can find meaning in an absurd hobby like running (or climbing, or surfing, or whatever), maybe you can also find meaning in another absurd activity called *life*.

50

SILENCE DOUBT AND KEEP RUNNING

Every once in a while, I come down with a pretty bad case of imposter syndrome. *You're not a real runner, Dave, so why are you even thinking about competing in this race? There's no possible way you'll survive!* Then the angel on my right shoulder whispers in my ear: "You've worked hard for this, Dave, and you deserve it. You can reach your goals, buddy, and don't let anybody tell you otherwise." So there you have it. My name isn't Thomas, but I'm quite a doubter.

You are a runner.

You are a runner because you ran.

You don't have to earn a degree to be a runner.

Or apply for a license.

Or pass a test.

Or give an oath.

You ran. That's good enough.

You're now an official member of the running community.

Welcome to the 'hood.

Talk about camaraderie. This is the same spirit that Paul enjoins on his readers in his letter to the Philippians. We run the race of life *together*. Of all the things I'm thankful for at this stage in life, it's the connection I have with friends and colleagues who are right there for me anytime I need them. And nothing has connected us and reconnected us more than honesty, than taking responsibility, than seeing our very souls as intertwined and seeing our lives as gifts we can give each other.

I am determined by God's grace to transform myself into the kind of man who would put the interests of my fellow runners over my own. Running taps into all the fears I have about myself. But it also holds the potential to tap into something vastly more important and beautiful.

The amount of grace that life requires is unfathomable. Let's allow the Lord to fill our containers to the brim this week — pushing through exhaustion like a marathoner and wrapping our arms around each other's necks when we have to.

5 1

ACCEPT THE GOOD AND THE BAD

I'm a firm believer in balance. Yes, I run, yes, I train, but I also teach and write and bike and climb and lift weights and blog and spend time with the family and sleep. I try to eat "clean" but I'm not an über-freak about my diet and will never eat food only from the local whole foods store. I don't believe in the "perfect" life.

That's one problem I have with so much modern worship music. It's so often just happy-happy-happy, Jesus-Jesus-Jesus. There's so little nuance. It's all white without any gray or black. As a musician, I'll add that, in my opinion, modern worship music has plenty of light (truth) but very little salt (attractiveness, beauty, artistry, musicality). Once again, the whole Christian music industry seems to be out of kilter, out of "balance" if you will.

Look at nature. After every fall comes winter, and every winter leads to spring and summer. It's an annual reminder that a similar dance awaits you and me. Light is balanced with darkness, fruitfulness with periods of barrenness. It's all a part of the natural life cycle. And the best news of all is that one day, maybe soon, the spring of springs will burst forth and we'll finally stand before our Lord, our Savior, the King of kings.

But for now, let's accept the good with the bad, the sorrow along with the joy, the happy days with the not-so happy days.

52

THE ULTIMATE METAPHOR

I love these quotes from the movie *Spirit of the Marathon*:

"Sometimes the moments that challenge us the most, define us the most."

"When you cross that finish line, no matter how slow or how fast, it will change your life forever."

"It's a scary distance."

"That's what the marathon teaches you. It teaches you to keep going."

"People run the marathon to prove that there's still triumph, that there's still possibility, in their life."

"The marathon is every man's Everest."

26 miles and 285 yards. An inconceivable distance. No other competition is like it. Basically, it's up to you. How dedicated you are. How willing you are to work. If your body can take it. Plus the sheer grace of God.

A marathon is the ultimate metaphor for any major undertaking in life. Does it hurt? Yes. Does it require time, effort, and commitment? Yes. But the payoff is out of this world. It doesn't matter what your goal is. Marathoner. Healthy eater. Patient mom. Writer. More diligent student. Divorce survivor. Whatever. You've got to push out of your self-imposed boundaries and never look back.

Life isn't as simple as saying, "I'm going to overcome this obstacle in my life." You have to actually deal with it. You take a deep breath and go one step at a time. Remember that you have weaknesses just like everybody else. Cliché as it sounds, there is so much value in sucking it up and just keep going on. When we have to, we can all do hard things.

Right now, as you read this book, there are millions of Americans who want to run a marathon but they're only dreaming. They aren't doing it. When I stood at the start of my first marathon, I realized that I was trying something that 99 percent of the population has never tried. You don't dream your way into the marathon club. You earn it. Once they place that medal around your neck, it becomes a symbol of your willingness to not only dream big, but to act on your dream.

In the words of John Bingham in the movie *Spirit of the Marathon*, "Some people *compete* in marathons. Others *complete* marathons. But the beauty is that the sport is big enough to embrace us all."

Amen and amen.

EPILOGUE

When the Roman poet Cicero had grown old, he wrote, "My soul seemed to understand that its true life would only begin after my death." Since Becky passed away 5 years ago, I've begun to understand what the ancient poet was trying to say. To lose one's wife after 37 years of marriage involves a death to self, to all the dreams you had of growing old together, to the intimate fellowship you enjoyed not only as husband and wife but as brother and sister in Christ. Her passing forced me to confront my fears and sense of helplessness. But it also enabled me to see the presence of God in that place of loneliness and sorrow. It is He and not running that has erased my grief and given me peace. But running, in small ways at least, has been and will remain a large part of my recovery. I'm not even sure how it all works. God simply uses the stuff of ordinary life to mold me into the man He wants me to become. Three changes come to mind immediately.

First of all, I am more dedicated to taking care of the temple God allows me to live in day in and day out. Life is, or should be, a struggle against complacency and self-indulgence. Neither a high income nor a college degree is required to adopt a healthy lifestyle. You just have to stay active. When I run, I join the athletes of ancient Greece who found their creativity in similar if not identical circumstances. I'm able to say with the apostle Paul, as it were, "No sloughing off for me. I have a race to run, and I'm going to do my best to finish it."

Secondly, I haven't stopped loving. I have too wonderful a family for me to ever do that. Honestly, despite the pain of separation from Becky, I have found immense joy in taking care of my family as a single father. I hope to become better at it as the years go by.

Finally, by taking up the sport of running, I've been reminded that all of us are here on this earth for a purpose. Have I fulfilled mine? A race is a litmus test for life. Judging from my upcoming race schedule, I apparently still have a lot of living to do.

As I type this epilogue, I've decided it's time to have another full body exam (including another stress test) in order to reevaluate my physical condition after 4 years of running. Being as active as I am is like taking a car that normally drives to the grocery store on a trip to California. When you're on the road you don't want unexpected mechanical surprises from previously hidden problems. Training *properly* is essential. The fact is, you can become involved in the sport of running and never once think about its risks to your cardiovascular system, for example. Which is odd when you think about it. There are about 100 million total runners in the U.S. today (of all levels and abilities). 94 percent of us are college educated. And yet we can train, exercise, and compete and at the same time lose aerobic health. We never think about scaling back, going slower, or running just for the fun of it. We like to "conquer." Running for us is a personal challenge. And there's nothing in the world wrong with that. The problem is that we don't always run *wisely*.

For example, my tendency at the end of a marathon is to sprint the last half mile to the finish line. That's actually one of the worst things you can do. Ever heard of the word "syncope"? Syncope is the medical term for blackout. When you run, your blood pools in your lower extremities. The blood vessels in your legs have to open up in order to carry oxygen-rich blood to your leg muscles. And if you push too hard at the end of a race or fail to keep walking after you cross the finish line, the blood collected in your legs means less blood available to your brain. The result can be "exercise-associated collapse." Not good. Here's another example. During several marathons I would take two Ibuprofen tablets about midway during the race. Little did I know that anti-inflammatory drugs like Advil, Ibuprofen, and Aleve have proven to be a risk factor for hyponatremia — low sodium level and high cellular water level. Another big no-no.

Like many of you, I've always been an ambitious goal-setter. I thrive on accomplishing difficult tasks and using Big Hairy Audacious Goals as stepping stones to another. But marathoners need to be grounded in reality. As I've often said, the Greek ideal was moderation. (The Greek saying is "Nothing in excess.") It means adhering to a workout and exercise program that's the best possible one for you. And the appropriate regimen is something that only you can figure out for yourself. Our fetish for fitness in America can lead to unwanted consequences. As with Aesop's famous story about the tortoise and the hare, it's all about being "slow" and "steady." Runners may be fit, but we're not invulnerable. Running injuries are not due to running. They're due to subtle structural anomalies in your body. That's why it's time for me to do another round of testing. Are there structural weaknesses in my body that I've overlooked? Have I fallen prey to the overuse syndrome? Seeing a sports physiologist can help me answer the age-old question: How fast should I go and how frequently should the activity be performed? Exercise can guarantee fitness but it can't guarantee good health. We can stay healthy only if we take care of our body as we would the cars we drive every day.

I've discovered I'm a risk-taker, perhaps too much so. Yes, I need to be challenged. I need to find out how much effort I can put out, what I can endure, if I measure up. But if a fitness program is to succeed, it must promote good health.

Words will never be able to express what running has meant to me. I wish that every man and woman could experience what I have, though without the pain of loss. It's easier to grow older if we are neither bored nor boring. Exercise is vital to our mental, physical, and spiritual health, and there is no limit to realizing our God-given potential. That great "cloud of witnesses" who now rest from their labors, and are never really separated from us, are cheering us on.